Current
CONTROVERSIES

Microaggressions, Safe Spaces, and Trigger Warnings

Other Books in the Current Controversies Series

Current
CONTROVERSIES

Microaggressions, Safe Spaces, and Trigger Warnings

Gary Wiener, Book Editor

GREENHAVEN PUBLISHING

Published in 2018 by Greenhaven Publishing, LLC
353 3rd Avenue, Suite 255, New York, NY 10010

Copyright © 2018 by Greenhaven Publishing, LLC

First Edition

Articles in Greenhaven Publishing anthologies are often edited for length to meet page
requirements. In addition, original titles of these works are changed to clearly present
the main thesis and to explicitly indicate the author's opinion. Every effort is made to
ensure that Greenhaven Publishing accurately reflects the original intent of the authors.
Every effort has been made to trace the owners of the copyrighted material.

Cover image: ESB Professional/Shutterstock.com

Library of Congress Cataloging-in-Publication Data

Names: Wiener, Gary (Book editor), editor.
Title: Microaggressions, safe spaces, and trigger warnings / Gary Wiener,
  book editor.
Description: First edition. | New York : Greenhaven Publishing, 2018. |
  Series: Current controversies | Includes bibliographical references and
  index. | Audience: Grades 9-12.
Identifiers: LCCN 2017040710| ISBN 9781534502369 (library bound) | ISBN
  9781534502420 (pbk.)
Subjects: LCSH: Cultural pluralism--United States--Juvenile literature. |
  Minorities--United States--Juvenile literature. | Microaggressions--United
  States--Juvenile literature.
Classification: LCC HN90.M84 .M53 2018 | DDC 305.800973--dc23
LC record available at https://lccn.loc.gov/2017040710

Manufactured in the United States of America

Website: http://greenhavenpublishing.com

Contents

Chapter 2: Are Trigger Warnings Useful?

Yes: Trigger Warnings Are a Courtesy for Those Impacted by Certain Subject Matter

to use trigger warnings as an optional pedagogical tool to enhance learning.

No: Trigger Warnings Threaten Freedom of Speech

Joe Carter

Many are uncomfortable with the idea that colleges and universities are places of free inquiry and want to disallow speakers whose ideas do not support their own. Students should be taught how to navigate a world where many disagree with their beliefs and values.

American Association of University Professors

The idea that students need to be protected instead of challenged in the classroom is simultaneously infantilizing and anti-intellectual. Trigger warnings create an oppressive intellectual climate on college campuses.

Chapter 3: Are Microaggressions a Real Problem?

Caroline Toscano

What precisely are microaggressions and how do they impact a classroom environment? A teaching professional breaks down the concept with simple examples, urging fellow educators to think about what is often a "death by a thousand cuts."

Yes: Microaggressions Are Real

Jennifer Crandall and Gina A. Garcia

When it comes to microaggressions and microinvalidations, intent does not matter, only the impact on the marginalized person. The effects of microaggressions can be physically, emotionally, and psychologically detrimental.

Kevin L. Nadal

A barrage of microaggressions suffered throughout life can impede a person from accepting his or her gay identity. People need to admit it when they commit microaggressions, apologize, and learn from their wrongdoing.

When looking at the concept of safe spaces as defined from a community and event perspective, the pros and cons become clear—and, for some, it comes down to what purpose each type of space serves.

Yes: Safe Spaces Create a Refuge for Those Who Experience Prejudice and Bigotry

No: Safe Spaces Do Not Really Help People

Foreword

C ontroversy" is a word that has an undeniably unpleasant connotation. It carries a definite negative charge. Controversy can spoil family gatherings, spread a chill around classroom and campus discussion, inflame public discourse, open raw civic wounds, and lead to the ouster of public officials. We often feel that controversy is almost akin to bad manners, a rude and shocking eruption of that which must not be spoken or thought of in polite, tightly guarded society. To avoid controversy, to quell controversy, is often seen as a public good, a victory for etiquette, perhaps even a moral or ethical imperative.

Yet the studious, deliberate avoidance of controversy is also a whitewashing, a denial, a death threat to democracy. It is a false sterilizing and sanitizing and superficial ordering of the messy, ragged, chaotic, at times ugly processes by which a healthy democracy identifies and confronts challenges, engages in passionate debate about appropriate approaches and solutions, and arrives at something like a consensus and a broadly accepted and supported way forward. Controversy is the megaphone, the speaker's corner, the public square through which the citizenry finds and uses its voice. Controversy is the life's blood of our democracy and absolutely essential to the vibrant health of our society.

Our present age is certainly no stranger to controversy. We are consumed by fierce debates about technology, privacy, political correctness, poverty, violence, crime and policing, guns, immigration, civil and human rights, terrorism, militarism, environmental protection, and gender and racial equality. Loudly competing voices are raised every day, shouting opposing opinions, putting forth competing agendas, and summoning starkly different visions of a utopian or dystopian future. Often these voices attempt to shout the others down; there is precious little listening and considering among the cacophonous din. Yet listening and considering, too, are essential to the health of a democracy. If controversy is democracy's lusty lifeblood, respectful listening and careful thought are its higher faculties, its brain, its conscience.

Current Controversies does not shy away from or attempt to hush the loudly competing voices. It seeks to provide readers with as wide and representative as possible a range of articulate voices on any given controversy of the day, separates each one out to allow it to be heard clearly and fairly, and encourages careful listening to each of these well-crafted, thoughtfully expressed opinions, supplied by some of today's leading academics, thinkers, analysts, politicians, policy makers, economists, activists, change agents, and advocates. Only after listening to a wide range of opinions on an issue, evaluating the strengths and weaknesses of each argument, assessing how well the facts and available evidence mesh with the stated opinions and conclusions, and thoughtfully and critically examining one's own beliefs and conscience can the reader begin to arrive at his or her own conclusions and articulate his or her own stance on the spotlighted controversy.

This process is facilitated and supported in each Current Controversies volume by an introduction and chapter overviews that provide readers with the essential context they need to begin engaging with the spotlighted controversies, with the debates surrounding them, and with their own perhaps shifting or nascent opinions on them. Chapters are organized around several key questions that are answered with diverse opinions representing all points on the political spectrum. In its content, organization, and methodology, readers are encouraged to determine the authors' point of view and purpose, interrogate and analyze the various arguments and their rhetoric and structure, evaluate the arguments' strengths and weaknesses, test their claims against available facts and evidence, judge the validity of the reasoning, and bring into clearer, sharper focus the reader's own beliefs and conclusions and how they may differ from or align with those in the collection or those of classmates.

Research has shown that reading comprehension skills improve dramatically when students are provided with compelling, intriguing, and relevant "discussable" texts. The subject matter of these collections could not be more compelling, intriguing, or urgently relevant to today's students and the world they are poised to inherit. The anthologized articles also provide the basis for stimulating, lively, and passionate classroom debates. Students who are compelled to anticipate objections to their own argument and identify the flaws in those of an opponent read more carefully, think more critically, and steep themselves in relevant context, facts, and information more thoroughly. In short, using discussable text of the kind provided by every single volume in the Current Controversies series encourages close reading, facilitates reading comprehension, fosters research, strengthens critical thinking, and greatly enlivens and energizes classroom discussion and participation. The entire learning process is deepened, extended, and strengthened.

If we are to foster a knowledgeable, responsible, active, and engaged citizenry, we must provide readers with the intellectual, interpretive, and critical-thinking tools and experience necessary to make sense of the world around them and of the all-important debates and arguments that inform it. We must encourage them not to run away from or attempt to quell controversy but to embrace it in a responsible, conscientious, and thoughtful way, to sharpen and strengthen their own informed opinions by listening to and critically analyzing those of others. This series encourages respectful engagement with and analysis of current controversies and competing opinions and fosters a resulting increase in the strength and rigor of one's own opinions and stances. As such, it helps readers assume their rightful place in the public square and provides them with the skills necessary to uphold their awesome responsibility—guaranteeing the continued and future health of a vital, vibrant, and free democracy.

Introduction

While American society has, for the most part, grown more civilized over the years, with a corresponding decrease in overt acts of racism, sexism, anti-Semitism, homophobia, and the like, there is no doubt that such "isms" still exist and that offensive comments are common. Given the barrage of offensive language and actions toward minorities and marginalized groups, those affected have come up with ways to safeguard themselves. Such reactions have taken the form of trigger warnings, safe spaces, and the concept of microaggressions, which are all designed to act as a bulwark against a daily dose of insensitivities that are rampant in modern society.

Trigger warnings, which have a history of use online for those suffering from post-traumatic stress disorder, are a way of alerting those who have suffered trauma that they may be hearing distressing material in a college course or reading such material in a book. Safe spaces are designed to allow trauma victims or marginalized individuals to openly discuss issues affecting them without fear of a negative response. They may also be a shelter from general society where like-minded individuals can seek safe harbor. Microaggressions, on the other hand, are not protections but can be defined as those often random, often thoughtless, sometimes well-intentioned comments directed at a marginalized person. Telling an Asian American woman that she is intelligent due to her ethnicity might constitute a microaggression. Mistaking a black person for a service worker would be another. Praising a Jewish individual for not being stingy would be a third.

It might seem as if treating all individuals with respect and allowing for diversity would be a no-brainer, but recent efforts to call attention to microaggressions, to create safe spaces, and to warn people about potentially offensive or stressful material have come under fire. Many conservatives view microaggressions, safe spaces, and trigger warnings as political correctness run amok. They contend that these attempts to safeguard citizens actually limit freedom of speech and that they create a society full of what they derisively refer to as "snowflakes," that is, individuals who are so sensitive that a harsh word might cause them to melt away.

The debate over trigger warnings reached a new height in 2016, when the University of Chicago, one of the premiere institutions of higher learning in the country, sent a letter to incoming freshmen decrying trigger warnings and safe spaces:

> Our commitment to academic freedom means that we do not support so-called "trigger warnings," we do not cancel invited speakers because their topics might prove controversial, and we do not condone the creation of intellectual "safe spaces" where individuals can retreat from ideas and perspectives at odds with their own.[1]

The letter's author, Dean of Students John Ellison, says that trigger warnings and safe spaces hinder the free exchange of ideas on campus. While many in the academic community praised Ellison's commitment to academic freedom, he received much push-back, even from 150 University of Chicago faculty, who, in a letter of their own, distanced themselves from the dean's ideas. They argued for the value of safe spaces and trigger warnings, saying that:

> …requests [for trigger warnings and safe spaces] often touch on substantive, ongoing issues of bias, intolerance, and trauma that affect our intellectual exchanges. To start a conversation [as did Dean Ellison] by declaring that such requests are not worth making is an affront to the basic principles of liberal education and participatory democracy.[2]

In the microcosm of the University of Chicago, one can glimpse the contentious nature of the debate over protecting students that has been waged throughout the country. Proponents of trigger warnings insist that they are merely a courtesy and not an impediment to free speech in the classroom. In a *New York Times* article entitled "Why I Use Trigger Warnings," Cornell University professor Kate Manne states her case:

> The point is not to enable—let alone encourage—students to skip these readings or our subsequent class discussion (both of which are mandatory in my courses, absent a formal exemption). Rather, it is to allow those who are sensitive to these subjects to prepare themselves for reading about them, and better manage their reactions. The evidence suggests that at least some of the students in any given class of mine are likely to have suffered some sort of trauma, whether from sexual assault or another type of abuse or violence. So I think the benefits of trigger warnings can be significant. [3]

Conversely, in an *Atlantic* article bearing the provocative title, "The Coddling of the American Mind," authors Greg Lukianoff and Jonathan Haidt argue that trigger warnings, safe spaces, and microaggressions are symptoms of a movement "undirected and driven largely by students, to scrub campuses clean of words, ideas, and subjects that might cause discomfort or give offense." [4]

With such divergent positions among academics (Haidt is a professor at New York University), it is no wonder that the controversy surrounding the protection of marginalized people remains unresolved on college campuses and in society at large. The essays in *Current Controversies: Microaggressions, Safe Spaces, and Trigger Warnings* investigate how such measures are employed in real-world situations and whether they are effective or not. The viewpoints in this book present a wide range of opinions on the uses and abuses inherent in providing safeguards and calling out subtle bigotry in contemporary society.

Footnotes

1. Quoted in Leonor Vivanco and Dawn Rhodes, "U. of C. Tells Incoming Freshmen It Does Not Support 'Trigger Warnings' or 'Safe Spaces,'" *Chicago Tribune*, August 26, 2016.

2. "Faculty Respond to Ellison with a Letter of Their Own." *Chicago Maroon*, September 13, 2016. https://www.chicagomaroon.com/article/2016/9/13/letter-faculty-respond-ellison-letter/

3. Kate Manne, "Why I Use Trigger Warnings" *New York Times*. September 19, 2015. https://www.nytimes.com/2015/09/20/opinion/sunday/why-i-use-trigger-warnings.html?_r=0

4. Greg Lukianoff and Jonathan Haidt, "The Coddling of the American Mind," *Atlantic,* September 2015. https://www.theatlantic.com/magazine/archive/2015/09/the-coddling-of-the-american-mind/399356/

CHAPTER 1

Should Trauma Victims and Marginalized People Be Protected?

Overview: Empathy for the Marginalized Depends on Levels of Discrimination

Natalia Khosla and Sean McElwee

Natalia Khosla, a Yale University graduate and MD candidate at the University of Chicago, conducts research about the intersection of health, social injustice, structural inequality, and public policy. Essayist Sean McElwee is a policy analyst for Demos.org and has written for outlets like the Atlantic, *the* New Republic, Rolling Stone, *and the* Washington Post.

I s Donald Trump really speaking for a "silent" majority of Americans when he says that political correctness is a scourge on the nation? Or do most Americans deeply value tolerance and inclusivity? The answer to this question may well decide the election this fall, so we decided to crunch the numbers. The data suggests that like so much in our changing society, your perspective depends on where you sit. And one key source of this divide is perceptions of continued discrimination in our society.

To explore views about political correctness, we used the American National Election Studies (ANES) 2016 pilot survey, a 1,200 person survey performed in January of this year.[1] ANES includes two questions that ask respondents if they think society needs to change the way it talks to be more sensitive to people from different backgrounds or if society has gone too far and people are too easily offended. There are two slightly differently worded questions on the same topic that are each asked to half of the respondents chosen at random.[2] We combined the two questions and then examined people who said society needs to be "a lot" and "a little" more sensitive, and then separately those who said society is "a lot" and "a little" too easily offended. ANES

"New Research Findings: People Who Say Society Is Too Politically Correct Tend Not to Have Experienced Discrimination," by Natalia Khosla and Sean McElwee, Demos.org, June 1, 2016. Reprinted by permission.

also asks respondents how much discrimination they think there is against a number of groups on a scale of 1 to 5, with blacks being one of the groups. We combined responses of "a great deal" and "a lot" of discrimination, "a little" and "a moderate amount" of discrimination, and "no discrimination at all."

We find that those who believe society is becoming overly politically correct also tend to believe there is less discrimination in society against African-Americans. We also find they are less likely to say there is discrimination against gays and lesbians.

Twenty-eight percent of respondents (and 32 percent of white respondents) say that African-Americans face "a little" or "no" discrimination despite overwhelming evidence and personal accounts of blatant discrimination on a daily basis against groups based on their race, gender, sexuality, and other identities. One study finds that "John" will be offered $4,000 more than "Jennifer" for the same job. Another finds that resumes with white-sounding names are more likely to be asked for an interview than identical resumes with black-sounding names.

Somewhat unsurprisingly, there are strong racial divides on the question of political correctness, with whites more likely to say that "people are too easily offended": 71% of whites, compared to only 34% of blacks and 42% of all people of color agree with this. We also find that those who faced discrimination based on their skin color are more likely to support changing language norms, and this holds true even among only people of color (which ensures the result doesn't merely reflect racial differences in views on political correctness).

Optimistically though, these data indicate that the reverse is also true: those who recognize that there is a great deal of discrimination against blacks are more likely to believe society needs to become more sensitive.

Also optimistically, whites who recognize that there is a great deal of discrimination against blacks are much more likely to believe that society needs to become more inclusive than whites who deny racial bias.

The data are clear: those who acknowledge that discrimination exists and have experienced it themselves think society needs to become more sensitive to people from different backgrounds. Those who haven't, don't. The majority of people who believe society is overly politically correct, then, are likely speaking from their own lived experience: they may not have experienced discrimination or may not think it occurs much, so when people take offense, they believe society is simply being too sensitive.

These differences of opinion are certainly important, but at some point the question of how inclusive the dominant society must be to the concerns of different people will have to move beyond the realm of personal preference. The racial and gender anxiety shuddering through this election shows that this time may have come. The United States is becoming a truly pluralistic nation, with residents and citizens who have roots in every community on the globe, and more individuals are demanding to express their gender and sexuality as they feel it. That diversity can be our greatest asset as a nation, but only if we forge a common understanding of the discrimination that exists, and a language that works for all of us.

Footnotes

The ANES has conducted national surveys of the American public since 1948. It is widely used by political scientists. Leading political scientists Stephen Ansolabehere and Brian Schaffner have confirmed the accuracy of opt-in panels (their study examines a survey completed by YouGov, the same firm used by the 2016 ANES pilot study). The questions on the 2016 pilot related to race were formulated by a group of scholars whose expertise is racial attitudes.

The full wording of the questions can be found at http://electionstudies.org/studypages/anes_pilot_2016_qnaire.pdf. The two versions of the political correctness question are:

There's been a lot of talk lately about "political correctness." Some people think that the way people talk needs to change with the times to be more sensitive to people from different backgrounds.

Others think that this has already gone too far and many people are just too easily offended. Which is closer to your opinion?

Some people think that the way people talk needs to change with the times to be more sensitive to people from different backgrounds. Others think that this has already gone too far and many people are just too easily offended. Which is closer to your opinion?

The "Snowflake" Generation Is a Misnomer

Courtney Smyth

Courtney Smyth is a blogger, freelance writer, feminist, and psychology student. She contributes to the music and topical sections of Headstuff.org and occasionally gets involved in media campaigns on human rights issues.

Yesterday I was listening to the radio. I had just missed the beginning of a chat segment. As I tuned in, I heard the words "whiny millennial snowflakes and their safe spaces" in such a divisive tone that I could only sit and stare at the radio for a moment or two.

I had been planning on writing something about so-called "snowflakes" for so long, and this was the tipping point.

To understand how ridiculous the whole concept of the "snowflake" is, we need to look at the etymology of the word. While there doesn't appear to be any exact starting point for its popular use among the masses who seem to think that an entire generation of people are all whiny, are all useless and are all responsible for the state of our economy worldwide, I can recall the term "snowflake" being first used on Tumblr. Circa 2011, the words "special snowflake" were used to describe a certain type of Tumblr user who identified as being gender fluid, or demi-sexual. It became a term used to laugh at young people for having the language to express how they felt about themselves.

"Millennial snowflakes" started a trend of using neologistic terms to discuss, frankly and honestly, aspects of self-identity that previous generations did not possess the language—and, perhaps, the self-awareness—to express. For this reason, "snowflake" was used to shut down conversation straying from heteronormativity and strictly cis-gender identities. Older generations and conservative millennials were possibly just able to wrap their heads around homosexuality and the existence of trans people, but the language used on Tumblr at this time was a departure from the umbrella terms that were creeping into everyday speech.

These frequent online discussions appeared to make these more conservative people uncomfortable. On Tumblr, people were able to discuss freely their mental health states—depression, anxiety, bipolar, eating disorders—and although there were toxic corners of the site where people actively encouraged others to remain in unhealthy thought cycles, it was a place where teens and young adults could express themselves safely. A space on the internet where they could be with other like-minded young people. The term "snowflake" was at the time used to describe someone who "wanted" to be treated differently, someone who "acted" as though they were special, and invented reasons to be treated as such.

The neologisms used to describe this wide spectrum of gender and sexuality were universally ridiculed—a reaction which is almost to be expected when young adults and teenagers are involved. There is a wider, more toxic culture of teens being ridiculed for everything they do. Even the concept of being a fangirl is frequently used as a dismissive, colloquialism. With the popular appropriation of the term "snowflake" to mean *absolutely anyone* between the ages of 18-35, but also possibly meaning *absolutely anyone* who dares to express a progressive view, the roots of its original use to mock teenagers on a cult blogging site shouldn't be ignored. Today, "snowflake" is designed to shut down anyone who dares to stray from socially accepted norms.

Listening to that speaker whine about whiny millennials in their safe spaces made many things occur to me. First was that people using the term special snowflake have absolutely no idea where it came from and are subsequently throwing the term around with reckless abandon in an effort to quell discussions about things such as, oh I don't know, equality, feminism, racism, affordable housing, mental health...Pretty much anything worth talking about. "Snowflake" is dragged out in an effort to shut down debate. It has no other purpose now.

It's about as effective as saying "Your ma" as a comeback.

We typically see "special snowflake" being used most predominantly right after the user refers to someone else expressing a progressive view as being "butthurt." You would probably expect to see this term used in a classroom full of ten year olds, but it is often employed by middle aged, middle class men with nothing better to do. We are living in terrifying times right now, and there are people punching down on anyone attempting to be inclusive or generate discussion on some of the horrible things happening around the world. There are people who do not want the issues society facing to permeate the bubble in which they live. This snowflake nonsense is masking the fear these people have of ever attaining a world where people are unafraid.

This snowflake generation that is apparently too lazy to work or buy a house or start a family is future proofing further generations. We are talking about unfair working hours and unfair working conditions. We are discussing the implications of dealing with mental health issues in workplaces and education. We are striving for an inclusive society, and in doing this insuring future "special snowflakes" don't die at the age of 60 from stress-related heart disease. We are starting to call time on the ludicrous set up our ancestors left behind, and we are calling bullshit on the notion that admitting we might not be able to do something isn't lazy, it's saving us.

We are creating spaces for people to be safe in. There are those of us in this world who are not afforded the social luxury of being middle class, cis, heterosexual and neurotypical. So if wanting to protect other humans is classed as "whiny," then I'm proud to be a whiny millennial. And if wanting to thrive in a culture that is determined to talk down to anyone they perceive as different is being a "snowflake," then I'm proud to be one of them too.

Media Ignores the Mental Health Crisis in Today's Colleges

Hannah Groch-Begley

Hannah Groch-Begley is research director at NARAL Pro-Choice America. Her articles have appeared online at Media Matters for America and Broadly.

*T*he Wall Street Journal's Peggy Noonan criticizes the "Trigger-Happy Generation" in her latest column, adding to the increasingly wide range of media figures questioning the merits of "safe spaces" and "trigger warnings" on college campuses. But her attacks in particular reveal a troubling element largely missing from this debate: an honest assessment of the crisis of mental health support for students.

Trigger warnings and safe spaces, in theory, attempt to warn and shield students from material that might remind them of past trauma or reinforce a hostile experience. In practice, they take on many different forms, giving ammunition to both defenders and critics who often see them as overzealous attempts to shield students from reality.

In her May 21 column, Noonan places herself squarely in the critics' camp, labeling on-campus advocacy for safe spaces and trigger warnings as "part of a growing censorship movement." She specifically targets an opinion piece in a Columbia University newspaper, which described in part a survivor of sexual assault wanting greater protection after feeling triggered during a class discussion on the rape scenes in Ovid's *Metamorphoses*. Noonan argues that the world is an unsafe place, and that students shouldn't try to shape it into something more comforting:

There is no such thing as safety. That is asking too much of life.

"Trigger Warnings, Safe Spaces, and the College Mental Health Crisis Media Coverage Ignores," by Hannah Groch-Begley, Media Matters for America, May 22, 2015. Reprinted by permission.

You can't expect those around you to constantly accommodate your need for safety ... [I]f you constantly feel anxious and frightened by what you encounter in life, are we sure that means the world must reorder itself? Might it mean you need a lot of therapy?

Noonan is being flippant, but her dismissive joke actually points to a growing problem: colleges don't offer students enough mental health support, which may be one explanation for the growing trend of students trying to create safe spaces and safe texts for themselves.

May is National Mental Health Awareness Month, and the same day Noonan's column was published, a report released as part of the campaign found that millennials who work (which would include many college students) have the highest rates of depression of any generation. Last year, *The Washington Post* noted that according to recent studies, "44 percent of college students experienced symptoms of depression, and suicide is one of the leading causes of death among college students."

And victims of rape, intimate-partner violence, stalking, or sexual assault—which the Columbia University student Noonan highlighted reportedly was—are "drastically more likely to develop a mental disorder at some point in their lives," according to a 2011 Journal of the American Medical Association study, CNN reported at the time.

These students often don't have access to help, including the therapy Noonan blithely suggested. In 2011, the American Psychological Association labeled the state of mental health on campuses a "growing crisis," and they've continued to track the concerns since. College counseling centers, they explained, "are frequently forced to come up with creative ways to manage their growing caseloads. For example, 76.6 percent of college counseling directors reported reducing the number of visits for non-crisis patients to cope with the increasing number of clients." 88 percent of campus counseling centers surveyed by the American College Counseling Association said they experienced staffing problems due to the increase in demand, the *Baltimore Sun* reported in 2013.

Some see this rise in numbers as a partially good sign, as it indicates more students are aware of the services available, and that the stigma against seeking help may be diminishing.

But as of 2012, only 56 percent of four-year colleges and universities offered on-campus psychiatric services. Fewer than 13 percent of community colleges did as well. The services can't keep up with the rise in demand.

To be sure, not all of the students asking for safe spaces or trigger warnings on their campuses need therapy, nor are they all seeking these spaces because of a general lack of robust mental health service on their campuses. However, I know at least some of them are, because that's exactly what I did.

When I attended Vassar College from 2008 to 2012, I sought therapy on campus in part to recover from my own experience of abuse. The campus health services were extraordinarily helpful for me—until they couldn't be. Because I wasn't a crisis case (I wasn't dealing with thoughts of suicide or self-harm in any way, for example), they asked if I would be willing to surrender my sessions to students facing a greater need.

Given their limited resources, this request made sense, and I was willing to oblige. But the sudden lack of a regular, dedicated place and time where I did feel safe and could work through everything from daily frustrations to larger trauma was deeply noticeable.

So when my friends and I decided to establish a "safe space" on campus for students who identified as women, it was for me a direct response to the lack of the more formalized support system therapy might have offered. Roar, as we called it, met once a week for an hour or two on Sunday nights, and gave us a chance to express fears, doubts, and confusions. We discussed everything from minor complaints, to triggering texts that appeared in our classes, to assault and abuse, and tried to offer one another coping strategies—and sometimes just a shoulder to cry on. According to friends, Roar is still active on Vassar's campus today.

As my friend Alyssa Rosenberg notes in the *Washington Post*, "in a world where members of marginalized communities *do* experience regular slights and hostilities, there is really something quite modest about the hope that a few spaces can be made to feel predictable." For survivors of trauma that exceeds daily slights, that hope seems even more reasonable.

Providing students with robust mental health services would not eliminate everyone's desire for trigger warnings or safe spaces, but it would allow those who need that additional support an outlet beyond the classroom.

And media figures who seek to mock the students who are making these requests for moments of predictability and security in their lives should first ask if the students really have any alternatives.

We Are Becoming a Culture of Victimization

Jonathan Haidt

Jonathan Haidt is a social psychologist and professor of ethical leadership at New York University's Stern School of Business. His books include The Happiness Hypothesis: Finding Modern Truth in Ancient Wisdom *and* The Righteous Mind: Why Good People Are Divided by Politics and Religion.

College students on many American campuses are showing an extraordinary mix of fragility and anger that is puzzling to outsiders. The recent events at Emory University are a dramatic case: some students described themselves as being afraid and "in pain" after seeing "Trump 2016" written in chalk around campus. They went to see the president of Emory to demand that he take punitive and protective action. The story is now drawing international wonder and scorn. How can this be happening in the cradle of modern democracy?

A surprisingly complete explanation of what is happening at Emory was offered by two sociologists in 2014 who described a new moral order they called "victimhood culture." I summarized that article last September on my blog at RighteousMind.com, but that was before the campus protests began at Missouri, Yale, and elsewhere. The events of the last 6 months, and the long lists of demands issued by students at 77 universities, have provided stunning validation of the analysis offered in the article. I am therefore reprinting my summary of the article here at Heterodox Academy. It is essential reading for anyone who wants to understand the dynamics of campus protests. It is particularly important for current college students who are at risk of being turned into "moral dependents" by this rapidly spreading moral matrix. Here is that summary:

"Victimhood Culture Explains What Is Happening at Emory," by Jonathan Haidt, Heterodox Academy, March 26, 2016. Reprinted by permission.

I just read the most extraordinary paper by two sociologists— Bradley Campbell and Jason Manning—explaining why concerns about microaggressions have erupted on many American college campuses in just the past few years. In brief: We're beginning a second transition of moral cultures. The first major transition happened in the 18th and 19th centuries when most Western societies moved away from cultures of *honor* (where people must earn honor and must therefore avenge insults on their own) to cultures of *dignity* in which people are assumed to have dignity and don't need to earn it. They foreswear violence, turn to courts or administrative bodies to respond to major transgressions, and for minor transgressions they either ignore them or attempt to resolve them by social means. There's no more dueling.

Campbell and Manning describe how this culture of dignity is now giving way to a new *culture of victimhood* in which people are encouraged to respond to even the slightest unintentional offense, as in an honor culture. But they must not obtain redress on their own; they must appeal for help to powerful others or administrative bodies, to whom they must make the case that they have been victimized. *It is the very presence of such administrative bodies, within a culture that is highly egalitarian and diverse (i.e., many college campuses) that gives rise to intense efforts to identify oneself as a fragile and aggrieved victim.* This is why we have seen the recent explosion of concerns about microaggressions, combined with demands for trigger warnings and safe spaces, that Greg Lukianoff and I wrote about in *The Coddling of the American Mind*.

I want to make the ideas in the article widely available. It's a fairly long article, so I provide below an outline of its main sections with extensive quotations from each section. My hope is that you can read the text below and get 80% of the value of the article in just 7 minutes.

In what follows, all text is copied and pasted directly from the published article, [except for comments from me, which are in brackets.] **I have also bolded** the lines that are most important for understanding the phenomena described in *The Coddling of the*

American Mind. **The key idea is that the new moral culture of victimhood fosters "moral dependence" and an atrophying of the ability to handle small interpersonal matters on one's own. At the same time that it weakens individuals, it creates a society of constant and intense moral conflict as people compete for status as victims or as defenders of victims**.

Here's the full citation: Campbell, B., & Manning, J. (2014). Microaggression and moral cultures. *Comparative sociology, 13*, 692-726.

Introduction

Conflict occurs when someone defines another's behavior as deviant—as immoral or otherwise objectionable.... Conflict and social control are both ubiquitous and diverse, as the issues that spark grievances and ways of handling them vary enormously across social settings. Here we address changing patterns of conflict in modern societies by focusing on a new species of social control that is increasingly common at American colleges and universities: the publicizing of microaggressions. [p.693]… As we dissect this phenomenon, then, we first address how it fits into a **larger class of conflict tactics in which the aggrieved seek to attract and mobilize the support of third parties. We note that these tactics sometimes involve building a case for action by documenting, exaggerating, or even falsifying offenses. We address the social logic by which such tactics operate and the social conditions likely to produce them—those that encourage aggrieved individuals to rely on third parties to manage their conflicts, but make obtaining third party support problematic.** We then turn to the content of the grievances expressed in microaggression complaints and related forms of social control, which focus on inequality and emphasize the dominance of offenders and the oppression of the aggrieved.

We argue that the social conditions that promote complaints of oppression and victimization overlap with those that promote case-building attempts to attract third parties. When such social

conditions are all present in high degrees, the result is a culture of victimhood in which individuals and groups display high sensitivity to slight, have a tendency to handle conflicts through complaints to third parties, and seek to cultivate an image of being victims who deserve assistance. [See DeScioli & Kurzban for more on the urgency of appealing to third parties] We contrast the culture of victimhood with cultures of honor and cultures of dignity.[p.695]

Dependence on Third Parties

A) Gossip, Protest, and Complaint

Of the many ways people bring their grievances to the attention of third parties, perhaps the most common is to complain privately to family, friends, co-workers, and acquaintances. This is called gossip—"evaluative talk about a person who is not present." ... Both individualized and collective conflicts might be brought to the attention of authority figures asked to punish the offender or otherwise handle the case. **Small children often bring their complaints to adults, for example, while adults might bring their complaints to the legal system** (e.g., Baumgartner 1992). Explaining the rise of microaggression complaints, then, **requires that we explain the conditions that lead individuals to bring their problems before third parties.** We suggest that the same factors that increase reliance on third parties in general encourage the public documenting of grievances in particular.

B) The Structural Logic of Moral Dependence

There are several circumstances that make individuals more likely to rely on third parties rather than their own devices. One factor is law. Historically, the growth of law has undermined various forms of unilateral social control. In times and places with little or no legal authority to protect property, settle disputes, or punish wrongdoers, people frequently handle such problems on their own through violent aggression—a phenomenon that students of law and social control refer to as "self-help"... Legal authority can potentially supplant other mechanisms of social control, from milder forms of self-help to negotiated compromise and mediation. **Insofar as people come to depend on law alone, their willingness or ability to use other forms of conflict management may atrophy, leading to a condition Black refers to as "legal overdependency"** (1989:77).[p.697]

Similarly, a college or university administration might handle conflicts among students and faculty. **Educational institutions not only police such academic misconduct as cheating and plagiarism, but increasingly enact codes forbidding interpersonal offenses**…. But note that reliance on third parties extends beyond reliance on authorities. Even if no authoritative action is taken, gossip and public shaming can be powerful sanctions. And even those who ultimately seek authoritative action might have to mobilize the support of additional third parties to convince authorities to act. **Indeed, the core of much modern activism, from protest rallies to leaflet campaigns to publicizing offenses on websites, appears to be concerned with rallying enough public support to convince authorities to act.** [p.698]

Campaigning for Support

A second notable feature of microaggression websites is that they do not merely call attention to a single offense, but seek to document a series of offenses that, taken together, are more severe than any individual incident. As the term "micro" implies, the slights and insults are acts that many would consider to be only minor offenses and that others might not deem offensive at all. As noted on the Oberlin Microaggressions site, for example, its purpose is to show that acts of "racist, heterosexist/ homophobic, anti-Semitic, classist, ableists, sexist/cissexist speech etc." are "not simply isolated incidents, but rather part of structural inequalities" (Oberlin Microaggressions 2013). **These sites hope to mobilize and sustain support for a moral crusade against such injustice by showing that the injustices are more severe than observers might realize.**

A) The Structural Logic of Partisanship

Black's theory of partisanship identifies two conditions that make support from third parties more likely. First, third parties are more likely to act as partisans when they are socially closer to one side of the conflict than to the other, as they take the side of the socially closer disputant (Black 1998:126)… Any social tie or social similarity a third party shares with one disputant but not the other increases the chance of partisanship. Second, third parties are more likely to act as partisans when one side of a conflict is higher in status than the other, as they take the side of the higher-status disputant (Black 1998:126). [p.700]… But note that these campaigns for support do not necessarily emanate from the lowest reaches of society—that they are not primarily stocked or led by those who are completely lacking in property, respectability, education, or other forms of social status. **Rather, such forms as microaggression complaints and protest demonstrations appear to flourish among the relatively educated and affluent populations of American colleges and universities**. The socially down and out are so inferior to third parties that they are unlikely to campaign for their support, just as they are unlikely to receive it. [p.701].

B) Partisanship and Conflict Severity

[This is a long section on how partisanship leads some participants to magnify, exaggerate, or even invent transgressions that never happened]

Domination as Deviance

A third notable feature of microaggression complaints is that the grievances focus on inequality and oppression—especially inequality and oppression based on cultural characteristics such as gender or ethnicity. Conduct is offensive because it perpetuates or increases the domination of some persons and groups by others.

A) Microaggression as Overstratification

According to Black (2011), as noted above, changes in stratification, intimacy, and diversity cause conflict. Microaggression complaints are largely about changes in stratification. They document actions said to increase the level of inequality in a social relationship—actions Black refers to as "overstratification." **Overstratification offenses occur whenever anyone rises above or falls below others in status. [Therefore…] a morality that privileges equality and condemns oppression is most likely to arise precisely in settings that already have relatively high degrees of equality… In modern Western societies, egalitarian ethics have developed alongside actual political and economic equality.** As women moved into the workforce in large numbers, became increasingly educated, made inroads into highly paid professions such as law and medicine, and became increasingly prominent in local, state, and national politics, **sexism became increasingly deviant**. The taboo has grown so strong that making racist statements, even in private, might jeopardize the careers of celebrities or the assets of businessmen (e.g., Fenno, Christensen, and Rainey 2014; Lynch 2013). [p.706-707] **[In other words, as progress is made toward a more equal and humane society, it takes a smaller and smaller offense to trigger a high level of outrage. The goalposts shift, allowing participants to maintain a constant level of anger and constant level of perceived victimization.]**

B) Microaggression as underdiversity

Microaggression offenses also tend to involve what Black calls "underdiversity"—the rejection of a culture. Large acts of underdiversity include things like genocide or political oppression, while smaller acts include ethnic jokes or insults. The publicizers of microaggressions are concerned with the latter, as well as more subtle, perhaps inadvertent, cultural slights…. Just as overstratification conflict varies inversely with stratification, **underdiversity conflict varies directly with diversity** (Black 2011:139). Attempts to increase stratification, we saw, are more deviant where stratification is at a minimum; **likewise, attempts to decrease diversity are more deviant where diversity is at a maximum**. In modern Western societies, an ethic of cultural tolerance – and often incompatibly, intolerance of intolerance —has developed in tandem with increasing diversity. Since microaggression offenses normally involve overstratification and underdiversity, intense concern about such offenses occurs at the intersection of the social conditions conducive to the seriousness of each. **It is in egalitarian and diverse settings—such as at modern American universities—that equality and diversity are most valued, and it is in these settings that perceived offenses against these values are most deviant. [p.707]. [Again, the paradox: places that make the most progress toward equality and diversity can expect to have the "lowest bar" for what counts as an offense against equality and inclusivity. Some colleges have lowered the bar so far that an innocent question, motivated by curiosity, such as "where are you from" is now branded as an act of aggression.]**

C) Victimhood as Virtue

When the victims publicize microaggressions they call attention to what they see as the deviant behavior of the offenders. In doing so they also call attention to their own victimization. Indeed, many ways of attracting the attention and sympathy of third parties emphasize or exacerbate the low status of the aggrieved. People portray themselves as oppressed by the powerful—as damaged, disadvantaged, and needy. [They describe such practices going back to ancient Rome and India] … **But why emphasize one's victimization?** Certainly the distinction between offender and victim always has moral significance, lowering the offender's moral status. **In the settings such as those that generate microaggression catalogs, though, where offenders are oppressors and victims are the oppressed, it also raises the moral status of the victims. This only increases the incentive to publicize grievances, and it means aggrieved parties are especially likely to highlight their identity as victims, emphasizing their own suffering and** innocence. **Their adversaries are privileged and blameworthy, but they themselves are pitiable and blameless.** [p.707-708] **[This is the great tragedy: the culture of victimization rewards people for taking on a personal identity as one who is damaged, weak, and aggrieved. This is a recipe for failure—and constant litigation—after students graduate from college and attempt to enter the workforce]**

[Reminder: All text not in brackets is from Campbell, B., & Manning, J. (2014). Microaggression and moral cultures. *Comparative Sociology, 13*, 692-726]

The Social Structure of Microaggression

In sum, microaggression catalogs are a form of social control in which the aggrieved collect and publicize accounts of intercollective offenses, making the case that relatively minor slights are part of a larger pattern of injustice and that those who suffer them are socially marginalized and deserving of sympathy. **[The social conditions that give rise to this form of social control] include a social setting with cultural diversity and relatively high levels of equality, though with the presence of strongly superior third parties such as legal officials and organizational administrators... Under these conditions, individuals are likely to express grievances about oppression, and aggrieved individuals are likely to depend on the aid of third parties, to cast a wide net in their attempt to find supporters, and to campaign for support by emphasizing their own need against a bullying adversary.** [p.710]

Several social trends encourage the growth of these forms of social control, particularly in the United States. **Since the rights movements of the 1960s and 1970s, racial, sexual, and other forms of intercollective inequality have declined, resulting in a more egalitarian society in which members are much more sensitive to those inequalities that remain.** The last few decades have seen **the continued growth of legal and administrative authority, including growth in the size and scope of university**

administrations and in the salaries of top administrators and the creation of specialized agencies of social control, such as offices whose sole purpose to increase "social justice" by combatting racial, ethnic, or other intercollective offenses (Lukianoff 2012:69–73). Social atomization has increased, undermining the solidary networks that once encouraged confrontational modes of social control and provided individuals with strong partisans, while at the same time**modern technology has allowed for mass communication to a virtual sea of weak partisans. This last trend has been especially dramatic during the past decade, with the result that aggrieved individuals can potentially appeal to millions of third parties.** [P. 710] …As social media becomes ever more ubiquitous, the ready availability of the court of public opinion may make public disclosure of offenses an increasingly likely course of action. As advertising one's victimization becomes an increasingly reliable way to attract attention and support, modern conditions may even lead to the emergence of a new moral culture. [**In other words: progress toward greater equality and inclusiveness, combined with the enormous growth of administrators and other "adults" on campus charged with adjudicating complaints about verbal behavior, plus social atomization, multiplied by the power of social media, explains why charges of "microaggression" have emerged so rapidly on some college campuses just in the last few years.**]

The Evolution of Moral Culture

Social scientists have long recognized a distinction between societies with a "culture of honor" and those with a "culture of dignity".... The moral evolution of modern Western society can be understood as a transition between these two cultures. [p. 711-712]

A) A Culture of Honor

Honor is a kind of status attached to physical bravery and the unwillingness to be dominated by anyone. Honor in this sense is a status that depends on the evaluations of others, and members of honor societies are expected to display their bravery by engaging in violent retaliation against those who offend them (Cooney 1998:108–109; Leung and Cohen 2011). Accordingly, those who engage in such violence often say that the opinions of others left them no choice at all…. In honor cultures, it is one's reputation that makes one honorable or not, and one must respond aggressively to insults, aggressions, and challenges or lose honor. Not to fight back is itself a kind of moral failing, such that "in honor cultures, people are shunned or criticized not for exacting vengeance but for failing to do so" (Cooney 1998:110). Honorable people must guard their reputations, so they are highly sensitive to insult, often responding aggressively to what might seem to outsiders as minor slights (Cohen et al. 1996; Cooney 1998:115–119; Leung and Cohen 2011)… Cultures of honor tend to arise in places where legal authority is weak or nonexistent and where a reputation for toughness is perhaps the only effective deterrent against predation or attack (Cooney 1998:122; Leung and Cohen 2011:510). **Because of their belief in the value of personal bravery and capability, people socialized into a culture of honor will often shun reliance on law or any other authority even when it is available, refusing to lower their standing by depending on another to handle their affairs** (Cooney 1998:122–129). But historically, as state authority has expanded and reliance on the law has increased, honor culture has given way to something else: a culture of dignity. [p. 712-713]

B) A Culture of Dignity

The prevailing culture in the modern West is one whose moral code is nearly the exact opposite of that of an honor culture. Rather than honor, a status based primarily on public opinion, people are said to have dignity, a kind of inherent worth that cannot be alienated by others (Berger 1970; see also Leung and Cohen 2011). Dignity exists independently of what others think, so a culture of dignity is one in which public reputation is less important. Insults might provoke offense, but they no longer have the same importance as a way of establishing or destroying a reputation for bravery. **It is even**

commendable to have "thick skin" that allows one to shrug off slights and even serious insults, and in a dignity-based society parents might teach children some version of "sticks and stones may break my bones, but words will never hurt me"—an idea that would be alien in a culture of honor (Leung and Cohen 2011:509). **People are to avoid insulting others, too, whether intentionally or not, and in general an ethic of self-restraint prevails**.

When intolerable conflicts do arise, dignity cultures prescribe direct but non-violent actions, such as negotiated compromise geared toward solving the problem (Aslani et al. 2012). Failing this, or if the offense is sufficiently severe, people are to go to the police or appeal to the courts. Unlike the honorable, the dignified approve of appeals to third parties and condemn those who "take the law into their own hands." For offenses like theft, assault, or breach of contract, people in a dignity culture will use law without shame. **But in keeping with their ethic of restraint and toleration, it is not necessarily their first resort, and they might condemn many uses of the authorities as frivolous. People might even be expected to tolerate serious but accidental personal injuries…. The ideal in dignity cultures is thus to use the courts as quickly, quietly, and rarely as possible.** The growth of law, order, and commerce in the modern world facilitated the rise of the culture of dignity, which largely supplanted the culture of honor among the middle and upper classes of the West…. But the rise of microaggression complaints suggests a new direction in the evolution of moral culture.

C) A Culture of Victimhood

Microaggression complaints have characteristics that put them at odds with both honor and dignity cultures. Honorable people are sensitive to insult, and so they would understand that microaggressions, even if unintentional, are severe offenses that demand a serious response. But honor cultures value unilateral aggression and disparage appeals for help. **Public complaints** that advertise or even exaggerate one's own victimization and need for sympathy would be anathema to a person of honor—tantamount to showing that one had no honor at all. Members of a dignity culture, on the other hand, would see no shame in appealing to third parties, but they would not approve of such appeals for minor and merely verbal offenses. Instead they would likely counsel either confronting the offender directly to discuss the issue, or better yet, ignoring the remarks altogether. [p.714-715]

A culture of victimhood is one characterized by concern with status and sensitivity to slight combined with a heavy reliance on third parties. People are intolerant of insults, even if unintentional, and react by bringing them to the attention of authorities or to the public at large. Domination is the main form of deviance, and victimization a way of attracting sympathy, so rather than emphasize either their strength or inner worth, the aggrieved emphasize their oppression and social marginalization. ... Under such conditions complaint to third parties has supplanted both toleration and negotiation. People increasingly demand help from others, and advertise their oppression as evidence that they deserve respect and assistance. Thus we might call this moral culture a culture of victimhood because the moral status of the victim, at its nadir in honor cultures, has risen to new heights.[p.715]

The culture of victimhood is currently most entrenched on college campuses, where microaggression complaints are most prevalent. Other ways of campaigning for support from third parties and emphasizing one's own oppression—from protest demonstrations to the invented victimization of hate-crime hoaxes —are prevalent in this setting as well. That victimhood culture is so evident among campus activists might lead the reader to believe this is entirely a phenomenon of the political left, and indeed, the narrative of oppression and victimization is especially congenial to the leftist worldview (Haidt 2012:296; Kling 2013; Smith 2003:82). But insofar as they share a social

environment, the same conditions that lead the aggrieved to use a tactic against their adversaries encourage their adversaries to use that tactic as well. For instance, hate crime hoaxes do not all come from the left. [gives examples] … **Naturally, whenever victimhood (or honor, or anything else) confers status, all sorts of people will want to claim it.** As clinical psychologist David J. Ley notes, the response of those labeled as oppressors is frequently to "assert that they are a victim as well." Thus, "men criticized as sexist for challenging radical feminism defend themselves as victims of reverse sexism, [and] people criticized as being unsympathetic proclaim their own history of victimization."[p.715] [**In this way, victimhood culture causes a downward spiral of competitive victimhood. Young people on the left and the right get sucked into its vortex of grievance. We can expect political polarization to get steadily worse in the coming decades as this moral culture of victimhood spreads**]

Conclusions

The emerging victimhood culture appears to share [dignity culture's] disdain for risk, but it does condone calling attention to oneself [as in an honor culture] as long as one is **calling attention to one's own hardships – to weaknesses rather than strengths and to exploitation rather than exploits.** For example, students writing personal statements as part of their applications for colleges and graduate schools often write not of their academic achievements but instead—with the encouragement of the universities—about overcoming adversity such as a parent's job loss or having to shop at thrift stores (Lieber 2014). And in a setting where people increasingly eschew toleration and publicly air complaints to compel official action, personal discomfort looms large in official policy. For example, consider recent calls for "trigger warnings" in college classes or on course syllabuses to forewarn students they are about to exposed to topics that cause them distress… [**This is a clear link between microaggressions and trigger warnings—both make sense in a moral culture of victimhood**]

What we are seeing in these controversies is the clash between dignity and victimhood, much as in earlier times there was a clash between honor and dignity.... At universities and many other environments within modern America and, increasingly, other Western nations, the clash between dignity and victimhood engenders a similar kind of moral confusion: One person's standard provokes another's grievance, acts of social control themselves are treated as deviant, and unintentional offenses abound. And the conflict will continue. As it does each side will make its case, attracting supporters and winning or losing various battles. But remember that the moral concepts each side invokes are not free-floating ideas; they are reflections of social organization. Microaggression complaints and other specimens of victimhood occur in atomized and diverse settings that are fairly egalitarian except for the presence of strong and stable authority. In these settings behaviors that jeopardize equality or demean minority cultures are rare and those that occur mostly minor, but in this context even minor offenses—or perceived offenses—cause much anguish. And while the authorities and others might be sympathetic, their support is not automatic. Add to this mix modern communication technologies that make it easy to publicize grievances, and the result, as we have seen, is the rise of a victimhood culture.[p.718]

[So now it should be clear why the first response of some (not most) Emory students, upon seeing "Trump 2016" written in chalk, was to claim that they felt fearful and threatened, and to run to the president of the university, James Wagner, to convince him to act. Which he did, thereby validating their beliefs and strengthening victimhood culture at Emory. Trump holds views on race that are far outside of what was the mainstream before last year, so one could argue that this event is not a mirror image of someone writing "Hillary 2016." (See Conor Friedersdorf on this point.) But still, the students chose to impute the worst possible intent to the writer, they reacted in the most fearful way possible among all the available choices, even though none of the chalkings were threatening or racist, and they came together to demand action from the president, even though it was not clear that any action was needed. This is exactly the response that Manning and Campbell's essay leads us to predict from students who had fully embraced victimhood culture. Anti-Trump students who had not embraced victimhood would have engaged in "self-help": they would have simply erased the chalkings or written their own anti-Trump messages. Why bring in president Wagner?

At Heterodox Academy, we believe that victimhood culture is more likely to flourish when there is a lack of political diversity on campus—when there are no faculty members or administrators who are willing or able to challenge the political and psychological assumptions of the most radical students, and when libertarian and conservative students feel that they must keep quiet. We believe that exposure to viewpoint diversity, including political diversity, is essential preparation for life in a democracy. Universities that do not offer viewpoint diversity in their classrooms can expect to have students who panic when they encounter viewpoint diversity on their sidewalks.]

[Post Script: Campbell and Manning have published a new article in 2016 addressing many of the debates and questions that arose in late 2015 about their first article on microaggressions. Please see Campus Culture Wars and the Sociology of Morality.]

Americans Must Learn to Face Adversity

David Whalen

David Whalen is provost and professor of English at Hillsdale College in Michigan. He is the author of The Consolation of Rhetoric *and has published articles and essays on Renaissance poetry, nonfiction prose, and the history and philosophy of liberal arts education.*

What are we to make of higher education when students and institutions respond to the recent presidential election with cry-ins, canceled exams, therapy dogs, Play-Doh, coloring books, group screams, Legos, bubble-blowing, and trauma counseling? Well, college "ain't what it used to be."

For some time, higher learning has been a political matter, one where the primary aim is to usher students into the club of elite (supposedly enlightened) progressive opinion. Gone is the formation of keen, analytical habits of mind and rational argument.

The result is not just a poorly educated student body, but an infantilized one. Mature discourse is out, and fragility, dependence, and bad temper is in.

Rather than cultivate habits of sustained and sober thought, we encourage manufactured outrage and self-indulgent victimhood. Anyone who has spent time with 2-year-olds recognizes the behavior. In our case, however, we appear to cultivate it on our campuses.

An infantilized campus is bad enough, but it becomes intolerable when these are the places where leaders of a self-governing republic are usually formed.

Regardless of party or position, a citizenry incapable of facing adversity or unwilling to reason about and discuss difficult, public things will not likely produce leaders who can do so. If college campuses steep our future leaders in habits of entitled fragility,

"How Infantilized Campuses Threaten Our Nation's Future," by David Whalen, UnivForum.org. This article first appeared in the *Daily Signal*. Reprinted by permission.

the only politics they will be able to imagine is that of the tantrum.

Tellingly, this is exactly the kind of politics we have seen on campus, and, increasingly, off campus as well.

A darker view would regard our infantilized campuses as something more sinister than the accidental byproduct of politicized higher education. When the noise of a tantrum becomes a primary political instrument in place of reason, persuasion, and evidence, then volume, not thought, wins the day.

And volume is coercive. When 2-year-olds throw tantrums, they attempt to force matters and get their own way. A set of people taught not to reason but to huddle in safe spaces and throw the occasional tantrum is a people taught to impose their will. They have not been denied a voice; rather, they are intent upon being the only voice.

This is not to say that all post-election anxiety is necessarily irrational. But it is a lack of the aforementioned habits that makes aggression and extremism so common.

Genuine higher learning requires (among other things) time, intense application of thought, patient reflection, and maturity. Rather than an education in elite and coddled groupthink, real learning is an education in honed and sound thinking—thinking that is not victim to every fleeting passion.

This is precisely the kind of learning poet Robert Frost had in mind when he wrote, "So when at times the mob is swayed/ To carry praise or blame too far,/ We may choose something like a star/ To stay our minds on and be staid."

If we cannot restore the "higher" to higher education, if we cannot put down our Play-Doh and take up our Plato, it's unlikely we'll see a return of either to our politics or our learning.

CHAPTER 2

Are Trigger Warnings Useful?

Overview: Using Trigger Warnings Is an Individual Decision

Anya Kamenetz

Anya Kamenetz is National Public Radio's lead education blogger. Kamenetz is the author of several books about the future of education, including Generation Debt, DIY U: Edupunks, Edupreneurs, and the Coming Transformation of Higher Education *and* The Test.

This school year, the University of Chicago has put the debate over "trigger warnings" on campus back in the news. The University told incoming freshmen that, because of its commitment to freedom of expression, it does not support warnings to students about potentially difficult material.

But amid all the attention to trigger warnings, there have been very few facts about exactly how common they are and how they're used.

NPR Ed sent out a survey last fall to faculty members at colleges and universities around the country. We focused specifically on the types of institutions most students attend—not the elite private universities most often linked to the "trigger warning" idea.

We received more than 800 responses, and this month as the issue once again made headlines we followed up with some of those professors.

Here are some of our key findings:

1. About half of professors said they've used a trigger warning in advance of introducing potentially difficult material.

2. Most said they did so of their own volition, not because of a student's request or an administrative policy.

This was not a scientific sample, but it's one of the larger and more representative polls to be published on the topic to date.

Our sample included 829 instructors of undergraduates. Just over half of our respondents, 53.9 percent, said they teach at public four-year institutions and 27 percent said they were at two-year institutions.

These instructors were overwhelmingly familiar with trigger warnings: 86 percent knew the term and 56 percent said they had heard of colleagues who had used them.

But only 1.8 percent said, as of last fall, that their institutions had any official policies about their use.

Let's define terms.

The term "trigger" in this sense originates in psychology, where it pertains to people with a diagnosis of post-traumatic stress disorder. For survivors of combat violence, sexual abuse or other trauma, certain sights, sounds, smells or other reminders can bring on intense emotional and even physical reactions, like a full-blown panic attack.

In the media and elsewhere online, language similar to trigger warnings is often used more broadly to label material that concerns sexual abuse or sexual assault, that is potentially racially or politically offensive, or graphically violent or sexual. For example, when NPR covered the fatal shooting by police of Philando Castile, an African-American resident of the Minneapolis area, we included these words: "We'll embed the video here, with the warning that it contains images and language that viewers might find disturbing."

But the rules are different in a college classroom than in a therapeutic setting, and both are different than when addressing a general audience. Even some of our respondents who had supplied a form of trigger warning as a "courtesy" or "heads-up" said they didn't intend to give students a free pass to avoid uncomfortable topics.

In fact, the picture that emerges is of professors making private decisions within the four walls of the classroom. Only 3.4 percent said students had requested such a warning. Most instructors who told us they'd used trigger warnings—64.7 percent—did so because, they said, "I thought the material needed one."

So what are the types of material that are most likely to trigger a trigger warning?

Our respondents were most likely to say they had used trigger warnings in reference to sexual or violent material. Racially, politically, or religiously charged topics were mentioned less often.

"I have had students break down reading novels depicting sexual assault and incest in my gender studies courses," a professor at the University of North Carolina said in a survey response.

Joanna Hunter, who teaches sociology at Radford University in Virginia, told NPR Ed last week that she has given a warning before explaining the practice of female genital mutilation, within the broader context of a discussion of cultural relativism.

Lauren Griffith, a professor of ethnology at Texas Tech University, said that she gave warnings when teaching Native American students whose religious beliefs required that they undergo a form of ritual purification upon viewing images of death. However, she says, outside of such specific situations, she doesn't believe that trigger warnings best serve the cause of liberal education: "I think that trigger warnings can and should be used in a limited number of situations, but overusing them can create a situation in which students opt out of learning experiences simply because they don't want to confront their own assumptions about the world."

Hasan Jeffries, an associate professor of history at Ohio State University, said in an interview that heavy emotions—even tears —are parts of the learning process that he welcomes. He teaches African-American and U.S. history.

He tells his students at the beginning of each course, "This is hard history. It's hard to talk about, hard to absorb. It's filled with trauma, sexual violence, racial violence, visual images of murder and chaos. You may walk into my classroom and see an image of a lynching that was put on a postcard. This is America."

At the same time, he adds, he's sensitive to the fact that many of his students may have experienced, say, sexual assault or police violence in their personal lives.

"I understand and take seriously trauma triggers," Jeffries says. "I'm not hostile to one side or the other and I don't think there's an absolute position."

None of the professors we talked to said that they had had a student try to get out of an assignment or skip a class because of topics that made them uncomfortable. The most common response to a warning was either nothing at all, or at most, for a student to excuse him or herself from class for a few minutes.

Jeffries, like other faculty members, told us that his department had ultimately decided against issuing an official position on the use of trigger warnings: "The general consensus was, we're not really interested in putting those forward. We feel confident in ourselves as teachers and in the maturity of our students."

Trigger Warnings Are Not the Problem in Modern Universities

Bailey Pickens

Bailey Pickens graduated from the University of Chicago with a bachelor's in East Asian languages and civilizations and Yale Divinity School with a master of divinity. She lives in Connecticut, where she works as a hospital chaplain.

At the end of August, John Ellison, dean of the University of Chicago, joined the ranks of many an essayist penning searing critiques of something that does not exist.

Trigger warnings and their ostensible sidekick, the safe space, have featured regularly in the news and essays of cultural criticism in the last year, since protests at schools like Yale and the University of Missouri sent them rocketing to the forefront of the national consciousness. Piece after piece, by writers ranging from the quite conservative to the avowedly liberal and even the leftist, declares trigger warnings and safe spaces indicative of weakness of intellect, character, or courage on the part of students: these millennials are coddled, unwilling to engage with ideas in conflict with their own opinions, demanding that the university bend itself to their every emotional whim. In short, they are antithetical to everything the Western academy stands for.

If it were the case that trigger warnings were, in fact, "get out of discussion free" passes, or that safe spaces were meant to keep students from ever touching an unfriendly idea, then much of the frustration and passionate opposition coming from the academy and the unaffiliated intelligentsia would be warranted. But it is not.

The discrepancy between what trigger warnings and safe spaces *are* and what they are taken to be has already been pointed out. Kate

"Trigger Warnings: What We Fear," by Bailey Picken. This article originally appeared in Los Angeles Review of Books's BLARB (https://blog.lareviewofbooks.org) on September 26, 2016. Reprinted by permission.

Manne, a professor at Cornell, wrote in support of trigger warnings last year, observing of that "the point is not to enable—let alone encourage—students to skip these readings or our subsequent class discussion (both of which are mandatory in my courses, absent a formal exemption). Rather, it is to allow those who are sensitive to these subjects to prepare themselves for reading about them, and better manage their reactions." (It is telling that essays a year or more old remain as fresh and relevant as they were when they were penned: this debate has gone nowhere since it began.) As L.V. Anderson writes for *Slate*, Ellison's apparent misunderstanding of the purpose and effect of trigger warnings and safe spaces is a common one.

Conor Friedersdorf argues that this is not a misunderstanding, but rather that their defenders employ the original usages of the terms and their critics the "post-concept creep meanings" at play in "ways that undermine free inquiry," wagging his finger at defenders who avoid "acknowledg[ing] the excesses that obviously motivated [the critique], rather than treating them as straw men or bizarre, unrepresentative anomalies." This, however, comes down to battling anecdotes and epistemologies (where is the line between reasonable and bizarre?)—and conveniently brushes away the question of the usefulness of the pre-creep concept.

This brushing away is not coincidental. In a wide-ranging essay called "Against Students," again written last year when this debate was bubbling up, Sara Ahmed describes how good or useful things—concepts, protests, initiatives—can be cast as something undesirable or unreasonable and "swept up" in critiques of the undesirable or unreasonable, and how particular images of "problem students" are employed to do that sweeping work. "The 'problem student'" as Ahmed observes, is "a constellation of related figures: the consuming student, the censoring student, the over-sensitive student, and the complaining student." Ahmed goes on to describe how issues in the academy are made to reside in the bodies and persons of students: "Even if that failure [of students to act and think as they ought] is explained as a result of ideological shifts that students are not held responsible for—whether it be neoliberalism, managerialism or a new sexual puritanism—it is in the bodies of students that the failure is located": with students who are "consumers" of a commodified education, "censors" of free speech and open discussion, "over-sensitive" to issues of little import, and in all cases "complaining" in a way that throws a wrench in the operations of the university:

> *I was interested in how various points of view can be dismissed by being swept away or swept up by the charge of willfulness. So: What protesters are protesting* about can be ignored when protesters are assumed to be suffering from too much will; they are assumed to be opposing something because they are being oppositional. *The figures of the consuming student, censoring student, over-sensitive student, and complaining student are also doing something, they are up to something. These figures circulate in order to sweep something up. Different student protests can be dismissed as products of weaknesses of moral character (generated by "student culture" or "campus politics") and as the cause of a more general decline in values and standards.*

What Ahmed suggests is that the students being depicted in these pieces are not neutral objects: they are doing work. If Friedersdorf is correct that the rising horrified tide of antis is using post-creep terminology, it is nonetheless true that their critiques crowd out the issues of triggers and unsafeness, leaving much more cleanly drawn battle lines. On the one side is the liberal tradition, a Western academy enshrining "free inquiry" and vigorous debate; on the other, excesses and sulky fragility. When this is the proposed configuration, the faintly dismissive tone in which Jonathan Chait, again last year, inveighed against trigger warnings as part of a resurgence of "p.c. culture" is not only understandable but sympathetic.

Trigger warnings at their most basic are, in the words of a much-reviled Oberlin student, "trivially simple." A sentence or two on a syllabus is one option, a verbal heads-up ("The readings for next class contain graphic descriptions of rape/transcription of violently homophobic rhetoric/other; see you Wednesday") is another. Trigger warnings are not the same thing as safe spaces, despite them being invoked in the same breath more often than not. Safe spaces have been explained at length, but differ from every other affinity grouping (imagine: your church, your golf buddies, the people you pay the most attention to on Facebook) in their location (campuses) far more than in their purpose or function (emotional-social support and brief respite from the everyday grind of dealing with humanity at large, which may or may not "get" you). It is absurd to suggest that brief disclaimers and deliberate affinity groupings might bring down the entire edifice of Western academe.

The decibel level of attacks on "p.c. culture," trigger warnings in the university, and the very concept of a safe space on campus is bewildering within the confines of the debate as it is carried out — that is, according to the configuration posited by the academy's defenders. The requests described on the one (pro-warning) hand are so modest and the demands being bemoaned on the other (anti) are so unreasonable as to render the whole discussion too silly to merit tens of thousands of words. Yet the volume is less bewildering if we resist the casual "sweeping up" of the demands with the antis' depiction of the unreasonable student, if we lift it like a rug to look underneath.

John Ellison's letter to incoming first years declares that it is the University's "commitment" to "freedom of inquiry and expression," "engagement in vigorous discussion, debate, and even disagreement," and "academic freedom" that is behind its principled rejection of "so-called 'trigger warnings'" and "the creation of intellectual 'safe spaces.'" The free exchange of ideas is what makes the campus welcoming for everyone, says the letter. But the letter has just told incoming first years what kinds of ideas are not permitted on campus in order to create a campus environment in which the free exchange of ideas may flourish.

The University of Chicago's dedication to freedom of inquiry and vigorous debate is not an illusion or a lie. It encourages its students to engage critically with texts and with each other. Its unsentimental expectation that I would do more than regurgitate what I had read was the beginning of a sea change in me that, at eighteen, I could not fathom and for which I remain grateful. But there are nonnegotiable limits to what may be inquired about, debated, and criticized, and the university itself is outside of them. Ellison's letter is an attempt to re-cover the exposed borders of an ideal that is understood to be borderless. Any text, yes. Any other student, yes. Any theory, any idea in the abstract. But the foundation of the western university itself, by virtue of its place as the source and guardian of free speech and inquiry, should be exempt from inquiry. When the critical eye the University of Chicago and other traditional liberal arts labor to cultivate in their students is turned back on them, things get heated.

As the President of Brown University pointed out recently in her open letter, it is not the case that the college students calling for trigger warnings and safe spaces shy away from discomfort: the very issues they want to talk about publicly (rape, racism) make people "very uncomfortable indeed." And yet it is from these concrete discussions—about the liberal university's complicity in or indifference to rape and the perpetuation of institutional racism on their campuses and in the communities that surround them—that universities and their administrations most want to shy the moment they get too rowdy or too close to home. When students protest, administrators refuse to meet, hand-wring over civility, hide in their offices, and threaten to expel the student body president. The cancellation of speakers is a case in point: students did not invite the speakers and are in no position to cancel them, but when their vocal objection to a speaker's ideals—that is, *critical engagement*—becomes uncomfortable for the administration, the administration may cancel the speaker rather than confront a substantive disagreement. And then sweep their capitulation up with criticism of students' stubborn over-sensitivity. In the same way, this debate focuses tightly on trigger warnings and safe spaces on campus, without observing the ties between demands for more accessibility to the education offered on campus and demands for—to offer examples from Chicago—living wages for campus workers, transparency within the University's private police force, a trauma center at its famous hospital, and improved responses to sexual assault, lest the "problem students" seem to have larger, less self-involved agendas on their minds.

The western university is dedicated to freedom of inquiry and exchange of ideas, but these ideals are predicated on a host of assumptions that ruffle feathers when examined. Personal investment in questions, for instance, is widely held to preclude objectivity: if you care about something too much, if it is close to you in some way, then you *cannot* properly think or argue about it; "objectivity" (which, as any good postmodernist knows, is fake) is the thing. It is to the advantage of the University of Chicago, as synecdoche for the Academy, to imagine that the "vigorous discussion, debate, and even disagreement" that it treasures are without meaningful stakes. If these debates are just debates, then everyone can go home invigorated by the mental jousting and think no more of it. If these debates are not just debates, if they in fact are one end of a long strand woven into systems of abuse and oppression, then the university finds itself on rather more dubious moral ground. For the university to deny the usefulness of trigger warnings and safe spaces on campus is to insist that the university is somehow kept apart from the sordidness of the world around it, is not subject to the same forces, the same blindnesses, the same selfish interests, the same prejudices; that all ideas get equal airtime and implicit professorial support; that all of its students and faculty are somehow cleansed of prejudice when they arrive. It is to deny that students from different backgrounds have had different experiences, and those experiences may make the UChicago, or Yale, or Mizzou, or any other college experience substantively easier or more difficult. It is to deny that the particularity of the human can, or should, affect one's education beyond providing "diverse" aesthetics and perhaps "interesting" perspectives to "contribute" to the "discussion." It is to deny the possibility that the university is not an unmitigated force for good in the world—that it may in fact both do good and be part of the problem. It is to refuse to consider that the university may need to change in many of the same ways as the society around it, that it may in fact be subject to real criticism by people who, until relatively recently, could not attend at all.

Universities and defenders of capital-L Liberalism—those who worship at the feet of Free Speech and Not Getting Unreasonably Offended—oppose trigger warnings and safe spaces like some people vote for Trump: instinctive defensiveness of a treasured good and deep anxiety over the continued viability of that good—the university itself; over their own power to create and maintain a cultural environment; over the goodness of what they have given their lives to; over instability of what has seemed bedrock. It is not trigger warnings or safe spaces or protests over speakers that are the problem, it is the implication that the university as it is simply isn't *enough*, that the values at its core are relative and not absolute, that it might not be able to withstand truly critical inquiry into its mechanism and its priorities. And yet the education that the University of Chicago, and Yale, and their peer institutions are selling, one that broadens the mind, sharpens the thought, and deepens humanity, is precisely the kind of education that ought to benefit from vigorous debate over how it should be carried out. If the inviolability of the present model—one that was perfected when there was almost no one in the desks but white boys from families of means—is an ironclad presupposition, then no debate can be had, and craven letters to hopeful teenagers will continue to be the preferred mode of its defense.

Content Warnings Lead to a Better Learning Environment

The Sewanee Purple *Editorial Board*

The Sewanee Purple *is the student-run newspaper of Sewanee: the University of the South in Tennessee. The paper's mission is to bring awareness of daily life and special events at the college to students, faculty, and community members and to investigate matters that concern the welfare and enlightenment of the larger community.*

This summer, Dean of Students at the University of Chicago John Ellison informed members of the class of 2020 that the university "does not support so-called 'trigger warnings,'" allegedly for the purpose of "[learning] without fear of censorship." Dean Ellison seems to be under the impression that trigger warnings, otherwise known as content warnings, are a form of censorship that keep students from coming across views that differ from their own. The Editorial Board of The Sewanee Purple wholeheartedly rejects this definition and ban of trigger warnings.

A trigger warning is defined by both Oxford Dictionaries and Merriam-Webster as "a statement at the start of a piece of writing, video, etc., alerting the reader or viewer to the fact that it contains potentially distressing material (often used to introduce a description of such content)." This is not our definition, this is an internationally recognized definition by academic and editorial standards. When you go to a concert, you will most likely be alerted beforehand whether there are flashing or strobe lights during the performance. If you have epilepsy, this forewarning can prevent you from having a seizure, because you will be able to adequately prepare yourself to leave if necessary. Similarly, according to the Medical University of South Carolina, 31% of rape victims will develop post-traumatic stress disorder (PTSD) at some point in

"The Sewanee Purple endorses trigger warnings, creating more open learning environments," the *Sewanee Purple*, September 14, 2016. Reprinted by permission.

their lifetime. If a rape victim is not forewarned that a book or a movie required for class contains a depiction or description of rape, his or her PTSD may be triggered by the content. This is a legitimate medical condition all too often not treated as such. If a professor notes in the syllabus ahead of time that a book contains a graphic rape scene, a student has the opportunity to approach the professor and discuss options that will not be medically harmful to the student without inhibiting his or her learning experience.

The use of trigger warnings goes beyond medical needs. There is a difference between being uncomfortable and being so disgusted or shocked that one is unable to participate. Students should be uncomfortable, pushed beyond their boundaries. That's the best way to learn.

But we should never be de-sensitized, and nor should we celebrate de-sensitization. When students are forewarned of potentially disturbing content, they are able to better prepare themselves to participate fully in class. Disturbing content can include anything from rape and racial violence to murder. More than likely, the student has to read the book for class in spite of this. It's not censorship; it's a forewarning. The Editorial Board would like to be clear that we do not consider opposing views to be disturbing, and that content warnings are not appropriate in such usages.

Dean Ellison additionally states in his letter that the University of Chicago "does not condone the creation of intellectual 'safe spaces' where individuals can retreat from ideas and perspectives at odds with their own." Intellectual safe spaces are not bubbles in which a student can hide from the outside world. Rather, at Sewanee, we have noticed an effort among professors to create environments where all students feel comfortable talking, regardless of their views. If there is only one conservative individual in a class and he or she is attacked by liberal classmates every time he or she speaks up in a Politics class, there will be a point when that student no longer feels welcome to speak in class, and will stop contributing. Any learning environment suffers when a student no longer feels like his or her contribution is welcome. "Safe space" is an often tossed-around, misunderstood word, but in its proper form regarding classrooms, it refers to when students and professors agree to open academic discourse where everyone's views are welcomed and challenged without personal attacks. Expectations of civility and being able to disagree openly do not seem farfetched or needy.

We do not believe content warnings and the creation of safe spaces lead to censorship. In fact, we have seen the opposite to be true. When both are introduced with proper usage, content warnings and safe spaces lead to a better learning environment. By empowering students to discuss difficult issues and opposing views without personally attacking each other, academic discourse and freedoms are celebrated rather than censored.

Trigger Warnings Are Most Effective When They Are Not Mandatory

Alex Morey

Alex Morey is a graduate of the University of Wisconsin Law School and holds a master of science degree in broadcast journalism from Syracuse University's Newhouse School. She lives outside Washington, DC.

The American University Student Government's (AUSG's) recent request that the university adopt a mandatory trigger warning policy may signal the beginning of an academic freedom battle between students and faculty at the Washington, D.C.-area campus. It may also represent the beginning of an uptick in similar requests by students on campuses nationwide. FIRE reiterates its long-held position that the imposition of mandatory trigger warnings poses a serious threat to academic freedom and freedom of expression.

As described in an *Inside Higher Ed* report today, AUSG announced the debut of its #LetUsLearn campaign via YouTube in September. According to AUSG's post, the campaign is "aimed at pushing for the increased use of trigger warnings on syllabi in order to make [AU's] academic spaces available to all students, especially those who have experienced trauma."

The move counters last year's unanimously-approved resolution from AU's faculty senate, which formally asserted that the AU faculty "does not endorse offering 'trigger warnings' or otherwise labeling controversial material in such a way that students construe it as an option to 'opt out' of engaging with texts or concepts, or otherwise not participating in intellectual inquiries." In the immediate aftermath of that resolution, AU's undergraduate senate

"Student Government's Mandatory Trigger Warning Request May Signal Impending Academic Freedom Battle at American U," by Alex Morey, Foundation for Individual Rights in Education, October 4, 2016. Reprinted by permission.

pushed through its own unanimous bill formally endorsing the use of trigger warnings.

In this latest video, AUSG President Devontae Torriente said that as part of #LetUsLearn, he has reached out to the faculty senate in an attempt to "meet and begin to bridge the differences in understanding" about trigger warnings.

"We want to work together to create a campus-wide definition [and] to continue to make our academic spaces accessible to all students," Torriente explains in the video. He adds that AUSG believes trigger warnings on syllabi should be mandatory so that students who need them in order to meaningfully participate in classroom activities are not excluded:

> The fact of the matter is, trigger warnings are necessary in order to make our academic spaces accessible to all students, especially those who have experienced trauma.
>
> In doing so, we uphold AU's commitment to academic freedom and allow all students to participate in the exchange of ideas and discussion in the classroom. Without trigger warnings, students who have endured trauma such as interpersonal violence or experience post-traumatic stress disorder can be excluded from the classroom, negatively impacting their mental health and education.

FIRE debunked the frequent assertion that trigger warnings are never required when we found and reported this summer that there are at least five institutions that do so. (We also said we wanted to hear from those who knew of other higher education trigger warning requirements, and invite educators to contact us via email at triggerwarnings@thefire.org.)

We have also written at length about the ways in which mandatory trigger warnings chill both student and faculty speech, and inhibit academic freedom.

In his 2014 book *Freedom From Speech*, FIRE President and CEO Greg Lukianoff predicted a rise in student demands for mandatory trigger warnings. He's pointed out that this could spell trouble for academic freedom, as professors may self-censor when they feel pressure from students to give trigger warnings. Greg told *Inside Higher Ed* last year that because professors cannot anticipate "everything someone might require a trigger warning for," it puts "faculty members in a kind of impossible position."

FIRE's position is that faculty should be allowed to use trigger warnings, like any other pedagogical tool, at their discretion. Making trigger warnings mandatory is an affront to a faculty member's right to choose how to manage his or her classroom and approach topics in the manner they think best, based on best practices in their field and their own professional judgment and expertise. As we have also frequently noted, banning their use outright could have a similarly detrimental effect.

We had previously noted one case in which the trigger warning-censorship connection was undeniable: In 2014, Oberlin College faculty objected to a mandatory trigger warning policy that admonished professors to "remove triggering material [from syllabi] when it doesn't 'directly' contribute to learning goals." Oberlin administrators subsequently promised to revise the policy.

FIRE hopes AUSG similarly rethinks its push for mandatory trigger warnings and that AU faculty remain steadfast in their commitment to upholding free speech and academic freedom at their university.

Trigger Warnings Are Unnecessary

Joe Carter

Joe Carter is a senior editor at the Acton Institute, a think tank located in Grand Rapids, Michigan. He also serves as an adjunct professor of journalism at Patrick Henry College. He is the editor of the NIV Lifehacks Bible *and co-author of* How to Argue like Jesus: Learning Persuasion from History's Greatest Communicator.

I n the early 1930s a student organization at the University of Chicago invited William Z. Foster, the Communist Party's candidate for President, to give a lecture on campus. Not surprisingly, the event sparked outrage and criticism, both at the school and around the country. In response the school's president, Robert M. Hutchins said, "our students . . . should have freedom to discuss any problem that presents itself" and said the "cure" for ideas we oppose "lies through open discussion rather than through inhibition."

On a later occasion, Hutchins added that, "free inquiry is indispensable to the good life, that universities exist for the sake of such inquiry, [and] that without it they cease to be universities."

A lot has changed in the past 80 years. Today, for example, a candidate for the Republican Party is more likely to be banned from speaking on a college campus than would be a candidate for the Communist Party. But one thing has remained the same: many students (and some professors) are uncomfortable with the idea that colleges and universities should be bastions of free inquiry.

Over the past five years we've heard a lot about "trigger warnings" and "safe spaces." Triggers warnings are written warnings to alert students in advance that material assigned in a course might be upsetting or offensive. And safe spaces are, as Judith Shulevitz

"Colleges Don't Need 'Trigger Warnings'—and Neither Do Christian Students," by Joe Carter, Acton Institute, August 26, 2016. http://blog.acton.org/archives/88719-colleges-dont-need-trigger-warning-and-neither-do-christian-students.html. Reprinted by permission.

says, the "live-action version" of trigger warnings.

A prime example, as Shulevitz, was when at Brown University. When a speaker came to present research and facts about "the role of culture in sexual assault," students at Brown set up a "safe space" equipped with "cookies, coloring books, bubbles, Play-Doh, calming music, pillows, blankets and a video of frolicking puppies, as well as students and staff members trained to deal with trauma." The room wasn't for people who had been traumatized by an actual assault but to provide comfort to those who were "traumatized" by those who were offended by the content of the speech. As one student said, she had to return to the "safe space" because, ""I was feeling bombarded by a lot of viewpoints that really go against my dearly and closely held beliefs."

Unlike many other elite schools, the University of Chicago has chosen not to protect students from idea they may find offensive. In 2014 UC appointed a Committee on Freedom of Expression to help the school develop policies for promoting free and open discourse. One result has been the letter that the school recently sent out to freshman students:

> *Welcome and congratulations on your acceptance to the college at the University of Chicago. Earning a place in our community of scholars is no small achievement and we are delighted that you selected Chicago to continue your intellectual journey.*
>
> *Once here you will discover that one of the University of Chicago's defining characteristics is our commitment to freedom of inquiry and expression. ... Members of our community are encouraged to speak, write, listen, challenge, and learn, without fear of censorship. Civility and mutual respect are vital to all of us, and freedom of expression does not mean the freedom to harass or threaten others. You will find that we expect members of our community to be engaged in rigorous debate, discussion, and even disagreement. At times this may challenge you and even cause discomfort.*
>
> *Our commitment to academic freedom means that we do not support so called 'trigger warnings,' we do not cancel invited speakers because their topics might prove controversial, and we*

do not condone the creation of intellectual 'safe spaces' where individuals can retreat from ideas and perspectives at odds with their own.

While many conservatives will cheer the school's bold stance, we shouldn't forget that too many Christian students want to be coddled also. A survey by the National Coalition Against Censorship found that many professors report offering warnings for the sake of conservative or religious students:

Many professors report offering warnings for the sake of conservative or religious students. "I used trigger warnings to warn about foul or sexual language, sexual content, or violence in order to allow our very conservative students to feel more in control of the material," wrote one instructor.

In fact, many respondents commented about warnings to address religious sensitivities. A respondent who teaches and holds an administrative post reports receiving "many complaints, some with parental involvement. These have mostly been religious objections." . . . Another explained that "the trigger warnings that I place in my general education Humanities course syllabus have to do with religious and moral content that might be offensive to persons who are zealous about their particular faith." Yet another observed that "the Bible ... is a topic that can offend both fundamentalists and those who are not comfortable with religion." There was even a "Rastafarian student [who] was very offended at my comparison of Akhenaten's Great Hymn to Psalm 104."

Rather than joining the left in trying to ban certain ideas from campuses, conservative Christians should teach their children how to navigate a world that often disagrees with our beliefs and values.

Trigger Warnings Threaten Academic Freedom

American Association of University Professors

American Association of University Professors (AAUP) is a nonprofit association of higher education faculty and other academic professionals. Headquartered in Washington, DC, AAUP's members work at colleges and universities across the country.

This report was drafted by a subcommittee of Committee A on Academic Freedom and Tenure in August 2014 and has been approved by Committee A.

A current threat to academic freedom in the classroom comes from a demand that teachers provide warnings in advance if assigned material contains anything that might trigger difficult emotional responses for students. This follows from earlier calls not to offend students' sensibilities by introducing material that challenges their values and beliefs. The specific call for "trigger warnings" began in the blogosphere as a caution about graphic descriptions of rape on feminist sites, and has now migrated to university campuses in the form of requirements or proposals that students be alerted to all manner of topics that some believe may deeply offend and even set off a post-traumatic stress disorder (PTSD) response in some individuals. Oberlin College's original policy (since tabled to allow for further debate in the face of faculty opposition) is an example of the range of possible trigger topics: "racism, classism, sexism, heterosexism, cissexism, ableism, and other issues of privilege and oppression." It went on to say that a novel like Chinua Achebe's *Things Fall Apart* might "trigger readers who have experienced racism, colonialism, religious persecution, violence, suicide and more." It further cautioned

"On Trigger Warnings," American Association of University Professors, August 2014. Reprinted by permission.

faculty to "[r]emove triggering material when it does not contribute directly to the course learning goals."

As one report noted, at Wellesley College students objected to

a sculpture of a man in his underwear because it might be a source of "triggering thoughts regarding sexual assault." While the [students'] petition acknowledged that the sculpture might not disturb everyone on campus, it insisted that we share a "responsibility to pay attention to and attempt to answer the needs of all of our community members." Even after the artist explained that the figure was supposed to be sleepwalking, students continued to insist it be moved indoors. (Jenny Jarvie, "Trigger Happy" at http://www.newrepublic .com/ article/116842/trigger-warnings-have-spread-blogs-college-classes-thats-bad.)

The presumption that students need to be protected rather than challenged in a classroom is at once infantilizing and anti-intellectual. It makes comfort a higher priority than intellectual engagement and—as the Oberlin list demonstrates—it singles out politically controversial topics like sex, race, class, capitalism, and colonialism for attention. Indeed, if such topics are associated with triggers, correctly or not, they are likely to be marginalized if not avoided altogether by faculty who fear complaints for offending or discomforting some of their students. Although all faculty are affected by potential charges of this kind, non-tenured and contingent faculty are particularly at risk. In this way the demand for trigger warnings creates a repressive, "chilly climate" for critical thinking in the classroom.

Our concern extends to academic libraries, the repositories of content spanning all cultures and types of expression. We think the statement of the American Library Association regarding "labeling and rating systems" applies to trigger warnings. "Prejudicial labels are designed to restrict access, based on a value judgment that the content, language, or theme of the material, or the background or views of the creator(s) of the material, render it inappropriate or offensive for all or certain groups of users....When labeling is an attempt to prejudice attitudes, it is a censor's tool."

Institutional requirements or even suggestions that faculty use trigger warnings interfere with faculty academic freedom in the choice of course materials and teaching methods. Faculty might feel pressured into notifying students about course content for fear that some students might find it disturbing. Of course there may be instances in which a teacher judges it necessary to alert students to potentially difficult material and that is his or her right. Administrative requirements are different from individual faculty decisions. Administration regulation constitutes interference with academic freedom; faculty judgment is a legitimate exercise of autonomy.

There are reasons, however, for concern that even voluntary use of trigger warnings included on syllabi may be counterproductive to the educational experience. Such trigger warnings conflate exceptional individual experience of trauma with the anticipation of trauma for an entire group, and assume that individuals will respond negatively to certain content. A trigger warning might lead a student to simply not read an assignment or it might elicit a response from students they otherwise would not have had, focusing them on one aspect of a text and thus precluding other reactions. If, for example, *The House of Mirth* or *Anna Karenina* carried a warning about suicide, students might overlook the other questions about wealth, love, deception, and existential anxiety that are what those books are actually about. Trigger warnings thus run the risk of reducing complex literary, historical, sociological and political insights to a few negative characterizations. By calling attention to certain content in a given work, trigger warnings also signal an expected response to the content (e.g., dismay, distress, disapproval), and eliminate the element of surprise and spontaneity that can enrich the reading experience and provide critical insight.

Some discomfort is inevitable in classrooms if the goal is to expose students to new ideas, have them question beliefs they have taken for granted, grapple with ethical problems they have never considered, and, more generally, expand their horizons so as to become informed and responsible democratic citizens. Trigger warnings suggest that classrooms should offer protection and comfort rather than an intellectually challenging education. They reduce students to vulnerable victims rather than full participants in the intellectual process of education. The effect is to stifle thought on the part of both teachers and students who fear to raise questions that might make others "uncomfortable."

The classroom is not the appropriate venue to treat PTSD, which is a medical condition that requires serious medical treatment. Trigger warnings are an inadequate and diversionary response. Medical research suggests that triggers for individuals can be unpredictable, dependent on networks of association. So color, taste, smell, and sound may lead to flashbacks and panic attacks as often as the mention of actual forms of violence such as rape and war. The range of any student's sensitivity is thus impossible to anticipate. But if trigger warnings are required or expected, anything in a classroom that elicits a traumatic response could potentially expose teachers to all manner of discipline and punishment.

Instead of putting the onus for avoiding such responses on the teacher, cases of serious trauma should be referred to student health services. Faculty should, of course, be sensitive that such reactions may occur in their classrooms, but they should not be held responsible for them. Instead, as with other disabilities, a student diagnosed with PTSD should, in advance, agree on a plan for treatment with the relevant health advisors who, in some cases, may want to alert teachers to the presence of a trauma victim in their classroom. The Americans with Disabilities Act contains recommendations for reasonable accommodation to be made on an individual basis. This should be done without affecting other students' exposure to material that has educational value.

It is probably not coincidental that the call for trigger warnings comes at a time of increased attention to campus violence, especially to sexual assault that is often associated with the widespread abuse of alcohol. Trigger warnings are a way of displacing the problem, however, locating its solution in the classroom rather than in administrative attention to social behaviors that permit sexual violence to take place. Trigger warnings will not solve this problem, but only misdirect attention from it and, in the process, threaten the academic freedom of teachers and students whose classrooms should be open to difficult discussions, whatever form they take.

Are Microaggressions a Real Problem?

Overview: Understanding Microaggressions

Caroline Toscano

Caroline Toscano is an education program specialist at the University of Minnesota who works primarily in the International Teaching Assistant Program as a teacher trainer and supervisor. She has a PhD in educational psychology and an MA in teaching English as a second language.

> *We need to realize microaggessions are unconscious manifestations of a worldview of inclusion-exclusion, superiority-inferiority; thus, our major task is to make the invisible visible.*
>
> *—Derald Wing Sue*
> *in* Microaggressions
> in Everyday Life

Introduction

Not so long ago in a college-level public speaking class, a professor decided to spark up her class. Engage the students by asking them to come up with a topic, any topic, weird or normal, and expand upon it.

One student took on the challenge and called out, "Urinating!" The professor decided to go with it.

"Great," she said. "Let see…where do people in the US go to urinate?" The class giggled away, then said what they thought was obvious: the bathroom!

"OK," the professor nodded, on a roll. "And where do people in *other* countries go to urinate?"

Lu, an international student, cringed when the professor said this. Other students started calling out, "In the bushes!" and "On the side of the road!" In her mind, she thought, *Hello, we have bathrooms in my culture too.* She felt deeply insulted that the professor and the class would think of her country as being "less civilized" than the US.

The above is a true story retold to me by one of my students, whose name has been changed.

When thinking about diversity in the classroom, chances are, most instructors tend to see themselves as good-intentioned, egalitarian and fair-minded people. They certainly do not go out of their way to denigrate others. Yet, there are instances when seemingly "small" things individuals say or do in the class can leave a long-lasting impression in their students' minds, which has prompted the informal naming of an accumulation of these practices as "death by a thousand cuts."

Such "small" things are known as microaggressions or microinvalidations, according to Derald Wing Sue, professor of psychology and education at Columbia University and author of the book *Microaggressions in Everyday Life: Race, Gender and Sexual Orientation*. In his writing, Sue delineates between the two concepts:

- Microaggressions are "brief, everyday exchanges that send denigrating messages to certain individuals because of their group membership" (xvi).
- Microinvalidations are "characterized by communications or environmental cues that exclude, negate, or nullify the psychological thoughts, feelings, or experiential reality of certain groups..." (37).

For Further Thought

*Microaggressions often times appear
to be a compliment but contain a
meta-communication or a hidden
insult to the target groups in which
it is delivered. People who engage
in microaggressions are ordinary
folks who experience themselves
as good moral decent individuals.
Microaggressions occur because
they're outside the level of conscious
awareness of the perpetrator.*

—*Derald Wing Sue*
in Microaggressions
in Everyday Life

Sue created a short YouTube video to address typical microaggressions and microinvalidations—"how [each one] manifests itself, how it impacts people, and what can be done to address it." In one of the vignettes, a meeting is taking place with a group of men and one woman. The male participants seem to be talking to one another, ignoring the female participant. When she finally does speak, one of the male participants checks his cellphone for messages.

When I played the video in my class of international graduate teaching assistants to discuss this topic, one of my female students nodded furiously and told her own story:

"When I was in a seminar, I was the only female in the group. When one of the other students was explaining his idea, I jumped in and said I didn't agree with him and why. He then acted like I was an idiot and started explaining to me again his idea, like I couldn't understand. I could understand all right. I just didn't agree!"

Other students in my class privately expressed relief at the realization that these small slights weren't just "in their heads," and that there was actually a name for it.

In fact, one of my students recalled feeling strange when an instructor told her, "You write pretty well, for an international student." Problem is, the instructor most likely thought he or she was paying a compliment, not lobbing an insult. How can we understand what impact our words *really* have on our students?

These responses have shaped themes Sue draws into a taxonomy of microaggressions in his book; for example: Alien in One's Own Land (e.g., saying, "You speak English very well" to an American-born Asian student), Environmental Microaggressions (e.g., committee membership is all or mostly white and/or male), and Pathologizing Cultural Values/Communication Styles (e.g., Dismissing a student who brings up race/culture in class).

In order to deal with microaggressions in the classroom, Sue outlines eight guidelines in his book: 1) possess a working definition and understanding of microaggressions; 2) understand the self as a racial/cultural being by making the "invisible, visible"; 3) intellectually acknowledge one's own cultural conditioning and biases; 4) develop emotional comfort in discussing -isms; 5) make sense of one's own emotions; 6) control the process, not the content; 7) do not allow the dialogue to be brewed over in silence; and 8) express appreciation to the participating students.

Experiential reality of our students' perspectives and ally building are two essential components of overcoming microaggressions, as well, according to Sue: "Stand personally against all forms of bias and discrimination," he says.

Sources

Sue, Derald Wing. *Microaggressions in Everyday Life: Race, Gender, and Sexual Orientation*. New York, NY: John Wiley & Sons, 2010.

Sue, Derald Wing. "Microaggressions in Everyday Life." [YouTube video]: https://www.youtube.com/watch?v=BJL2P0JsAS4.

We Must Combat Microaggressions

Jennifer Crandall and Gina A. Garcia

Jennifer Crandall is a senior policy research analyst for the American Council on Education's Center for Policy Research and Strategy. Her research explores institutional influences on access, equity, and diversity in education. Gina Ann Garcia is assistant professor in the department of Administrative and Policy Studies at the University of Pittsburgh. Her research centers on issues of equity and diversity in higher education.

I (Gina) recently participated in a diversity training focused on race and racism in higher education, an area I focus on in my own research. As I sat in the training, I felt invisible as the presenter provided numerous activities and resources that addressed a black and white mono-racial binary.

In that training, my experience as a Latina-identified woman was diminished. The facilitator was well intentioned, well informed, and well respected for his knowledge in this area and had not intended to make me feel as if my experience as a racialized person did not matter. Yet that is how I felt.

While I have experienced blatant racism and sexism in my predominantly white institution situated in a mostly white urban city where 2 percent of the population shares a common racial/ethnic/cultural experience with me, I spend most of my time processing these types of daily microaggressions, wondering if I am imagining them. I often ask myself, "Am I overreacting?" "Did that just happen?"

This experience is not unique. Many people of color, women, LGBTQ, and other "minoritized" groups—social groups that may not be the minority in number but continue to be systemically oppressed and excluded—on college and university campuses experience microaggressions on a regular basis.

Forms of Microaggressions

Pioneering researcher Derald Sue defines microaggressions as "brief and commonplace daily verbal, behavioral, and environmental indignities, whether intentional or unintentional, that communicate hostile, derogatory, or negative racial, gender, sexual orientation, and religious slights and insults to the target person or group" (5). Even further, Sue and other researchers suggest there are different forms of microaggressions, including *microassaults* (explicit, verbal and nonverbal derogatory remarks), *microinsults*, (subtle remarks about a person's minoritized identities that are insensitive, demeaning and rude), and *microinvalidations* (an experience that excludes, negates, and nullifies a person's minoritized reality).

My experience in a diversity training that excluded my racial/ethnic/cultural experience is an example of a *microinvalidation.* Although the presenter did not intentionally exclude or degrade me, the impact was significant and serves as a reminder that intent does not matter, only the impact on the minoritized person. While we focus on racial microaggressions in this blog, there are many more based on other social identities, such as gender, sexual orientation, socioeconomic status, and other minoritized identities (for more, see the "additional resources" section at the end of this viewpoint).

Microaggressions vs. Racialized Aggressions

Chester Pierce first introduced the idea of racial microaggressions in the late 1960s in the field of psychiatry, while scholars like Derald Sue and Daniel Solórzano have further conceptualized the idea in counseling and education, respectively. Within higher education literature, there are an abundance of articles outlining the ways in which various racial groups experience microaggressions on college campuses (see, for example, Garcia, 2016; McCabe, 2009; Minikel-Lacocque, 2012; Solórzano, Ceja, & Yosso, 2000).

In recent years, the term has moved beyond the academic journals of psychiatry, counseling and education into mainstream media (Buzzfeed, for example, showcased a digital photo project on microaggressions experienced by Fordham students and alumni). Its more widespread use has led to an increase in criticism, with some suggesting that racialized groups are too sensitive and unable to take a joke, as illustrated in a Fox News clip. Others argue that while Sue and colleagues suggest that "old fashioned racism" (i.e., blatant racism) is dead in the 21st century, there are a growing number of racialized aggressions, particularly on college and university campuses.

Garcia and Johnston-Guerrero suggest that while microinsults and microinvalidations are subtle and often unintentional and unconscious to the perpetrator—albeit still harmful to the target— racialized aggressions *are* intentional. Examples include graffiti swastikas written on residence hall doors, racial epithets shouted at students, and makeshift nooses hung on campus. When racialized aggressions occur, higher education leaders often act immediately, as they are blatantly oppressive, offensive and racialized. The same type of response is not always the case when people on campus experience microaggressions, as they are often difficult to name and identify.

Effects of Racial Microaggressions

Whether subtle or aggressive in nature, the effects of microaggressions can be physically, emotionally and psychologically detrimental. Sue and others report that racial microaggressions can result in harmful psychological and physiological effects such as anxiety, nausea, resentment, isolation and depression. On college campuses, the perpetual nature of racial microaggressions may ultimately lead to large attrition rates of all minoritized constituents, including students, faculty, staff and campus leaders. This claim is supported by decades of research that shows when racialized groups experience a hostile campus climate, it negatively affects their sense of belonging, cross-racial interactions and degree completion (see Hurtado et al., 2012 for a discussion of the research on campus climate effects).

The challenge for college and university leaders, faculty, and staff is that racial microaggressions are systemic, meaning they are embedded within campus policies, programs and practices, subjecting community members to cultural standards that normalize whiteness. Moreover, the pervasive nature of microaggressions makes them difficult to address and eliminate.

How then do we move forward in order to disrupt racial microaggressions while creating a more welcoming and inclusive campus environment for all minoritized groups?

Actionable Steps for Creating an Inclusive Campus Racial Climate

In presenting actionable steps for confronting racial microaggressions, we focus broadly on an inclusive campus racial climate approach. This approach assumes that pluralism, or the belief that people should coexist in mutually beneficial and respectful ways for the common good, is inherent in the mission of most colleges and universities.

Include racially responsive training for administrators, faculty, staff and student leaders that explicitly addresses race and racism

It is difficult to respond to racial microaggressions, as both microaggressors and targets of microaggressions can lack the critical consciousness to recognize them, let alone disrupt and eliminate them. The first step is acknowledging that race and racism is enduring in the United States, and that microaggressions exist as a result. Consider using a microaggressions framework as a tool for offering a common language and a nuanced understanding of microaggressions. Training should also have administrators, faculty, staff and student leaders examine their own biases and prejudices to raise awareness and understanding of racism generally, but specifically among the majority population. Recognizing our own biases and prejudices is a first step towards limiting the occurrence of racial microaggressions.

Support co-curricular opportunities for students that have a meaningful effect on campus racial climate

This includes supporting student activism for racial and social change in addition to the development of campus communities where all constituents understand and learn about the racial and cultural wealth inherent within minoritized communities. Incentivizing faculty or staff to lead or advise students could further facilitate such co-curricular activities. A recent *Higher Education Today* blog on student activism suggests that it promotes critical thinking, civic engagement and leadership and serves as a learning opportunity for campus leaders. Research also shows that membership in a community that represents students' racial and cultural wealth can provide an inclusive space that galvanizes students toward action against racial microaggressions. Intergroup dialogue programs, first established at the University of Michigan, can also promote cross-racial group conversations that lead to better racial understanding.

Assess administrators, faculty, staff and student perceptions of racial inclusivity

In light of recent student protests on college and university campuses that sparked lists of demands to campus leaders, institutions need to be aware of how knowledgeable campus constituents are about the campus racial climate and its effects on students' experiences. The University of California's Higher Education Research Institute offers a Faculty Survey and a Diverse Learning Environments Survey (DLE) that can assist campuses with assessing faculty and students' perceptions of institutional racial climate and diversity. The survey provides institutions with disaggregated data to evaluate its alignment between diversity efforts and campus practices. This is just one of many forms of assessment that campuses can undertake to better understand the knowledge that faculty, staff and students have about race, racism and other issues of inclusion.

Strive for "dynamic diversity"

Institutions tend to measure racial diversity by demographics or the extent to which they have reached the critical mass of racialized students necessary to reap the benefits of a multiracial/ethnic student population. While tracking numbers is a step in the right direction, this approach falls short in addressing the complex task of creating a sustainable, inclusive environment. Dynamic diversity recognizes the multifaceted relationship students have with their environments and offers four components institutions should tend to: 1) cultivate a positive racial climate, 2) attend to institutional history and context, 3) break down barriers to cross-racial engagement, and 4) nurture cross-racial interactions.

Empower cross-functional teams committed to addressing racially inequitable educational environments and outcomes

The Equity Scorecard, developed by the University of Southern California's Center for Urban Education, engages faculty, staff and administrators in a change process designed to create equitable outcomes for racialized students. Each of the scorecards' five phases uses evidence-based inquiry tools to assess programs, curricula and learning outcomes and can be used to examine the impact campus racial climate has on racialized students. The phases—1) laying the groundwork, 2) defining the problem, 3) assessing interventions, 4) implementing solutions, and 5) evaluating results—culminate in a scorecard with actions institutions could take to meet their goals in addition to criteria for evaluating progress toward those goals.

Evaluate degree of "inclusive excellence," or how well colleges and universities and their leaders infuse diversity, equity and educational quality into institutional missions, goals and practices

The Inclusive Excellence Toolkit, created by the University of Denver (DU) faculty to advance the university's commitment to inclusive excellence, moves beyond traditional measures of diversity, such as demographic data, and measures an institution's progress toward inclusive excellence. DU and other institutions have used the toolkit to measure progress toward diversity and to improve campus racial climate. Similar to the DLE and Equity Scorecard mentioned above, institutions need to first establish a baseline to know where they are moving from and where they need to focus their efforts to attain racial equity and inclusion.

While racial microaggressions are prevalent in colleges and universities, we have witnessed an increased understanding of what these microaggressions look like and their implications for minoritized groups. With the abundance of research and knowledge available about racial and other forms of microaggressions, and the tools available for understanding and addressing them—a few of which we have laid out here—time is now for campus administrators, faculty, staff and student leaders to educate themselves, address their own biases and move toward disrupting racism within our institutions. We can no longer merely work toward multiculturalism and inclusivity, but rather we must address the larger systemic issues that allow racial microaggressions to flourish on campus. Moving toward a disruption of the larger system of racial oppression will lead to greater inclusivity and equity for all.

Additional Resources

Williams, D. A., Berger, J. B., & McClendon, S. A. (2005). *Toward a model of inclusive excellence and change in postsecondary institutions.* American Association of Colleges & Universities: Washington, DC.

Yosso, T. J., Smith, W. A., Ceja, M., & Solórzano, D. G. (2009). Critical race theory, racial microaggressions, and campus racial climate for Latina/o undergraduates. *Harvard Educational Review*, 79:4, 659-690.

Young, K., Anderson, M., & Stewart, S. (2015). Hierarchical Microaggressions in Higher Education. *Journal of Diversity in Higher Education*, 8: 1, 61-71.

Microaggressions Are Harmful to the LGBTQ Community

Kevin L. Nadal

Kevin L. Nadal teaches at the John Jay College of Criminal Justice. His books include That's So Gay! Microaggressions and the Lesbian, Gay, Bisexual, and Transgender Community *and* Filipino American Psychology: A Handbook of Theory, Research, and Clinical Practice.

When I was a little kid, I used to hear my brothers, cousins, and friends say things like "That's so gay!" on a pretty regular basis. I would usually laugh along, hoping with all my might that they didn't know my secret. My parents and other adults in my life would tell me things like "Boys don't cry" or "Be a man!" which essentially was their way of telling me that being emotional was forbidden or a sign of weakness.

When I was a teenager, there were a few boys at my high school who ridiculed me, almost everyday. When I walked by them in the halls, they called me a "faggot" or screamed my name in a flamboyant tone. I learned to walk by without showing any reaction; I could not let them know that it bothered me, or else I would be proving to them that I was indeed gay. I didn't tell anyone about the bullying (not my parents, teachers, or anyone) because admitting that I was being teased for being gay would mean that I was admitting to being gay. I had never felt so alone in my life.

In college, it got a little better. While I was no longer harassed about my closeted sexual orientation, I didn't have any friends that were openly gay and most of my friends didn't have any either. Some of my friends and family members still made occasional homophobic jokes in front of me. While many loved ones later told me that they suspected that I was gay, no one gave me any reason to believe that they were gay-friendly. So I just remained in the closet a few more years until I couldn't take it any more.

In retrospect, I had a very difficult time accepting my gay identity, because of the microaggressions that I experienced throughout my life. **Microaggressions are the everyday encounters of subtle discrimination that people of various marginalized groups experience throughout their lives** (Sue et al., 2007). Some microaggressions are unconscious (i.e., the perpetrator doesn't even know they did something) while some microaggressions may be unintentional (i.e., the perpetrator may be aware of their actions, but may not realize the negative impact they may have on people).

One of the reasons why it was important for me to study microaggressions against lesbian, gay, bisexual, transgender, queer and questioning (LGBTQ) people was because I knew that this type of discrimination existed and because I hypothesized that they had a significant impact on the lives of LGBTQ people, particularly on their mental health and identity development. I collaborated with two fellow psychologist colleagues, Dr. David Rivera and Dr. Melissa Corpus, and we theorized the various types of microaggressions that affect LGBTQ people (see Nadal et al., 2010). For the past several years, my research team and I interviewed all kinds of LGBTQ people and they all reported that microaggressions are very common in their lives.

Here are a few examples:

1) Use of heterosexist or transphobic terminology:

These types of microaggressions occur when someone uses disparaging heterosexist or transphobic language towards, or about, LGBTQ persons. For me, it is anytime someone says "That's so gay" and "No homo" in my presence; for my transgender friends, it could be anytime someone says "tranny", "she-male", or other derogatory terms. In hip hop, it is common for rappers to unapologetically use the word "faggot", which then gives permission for kids to use the term unapologetically in everyday life. Maybe this is why 9 out of 10 LGBTQ high school students report experiencing harassment at school and why 2/3 of them say they feel unsafe (Gay, Lesbian, and Straight Education Network, 2010).

2) Endorsement of heteronormative culture and behaviors:

These kinds of microaggressions take place when an LGBTQ person is assumed to be heterosexual, or when they are encouraged to act in gender-conforming ways. I know that I've been told that I shouldn't be so flamboyant or that I should act "more masculine". As a child, my family forced me to play sports, yet sighed when I played with Barbie. As a young adult, when someone asked me "if I had a girlfriend" or "a wife or kids", they were essentially telling me that they expected me to be heterosexual. Heterosexuals don't realize that it is common for them to assume someone is straight, unless proven otherwise.

3) Assumption of universal LGBTQ experience:

These sorts of microaggressions transpire when heterosexual people assume that all LGBTQ persons are the same. For instance, sometimes, people tell me I'm not "a typical gay guy" because of some stereotype I don't fulfill; other times, people assume that I would automatically get along with another gay guy simply because we are attracted to the same gender. Lesbian women have reported that people presume that they should all be masculine, while bisexual people have reported that they are often stereotyped as being "confused" (Nadal, Issa, et al., 2011). Many transgender women have reported being arrested and falsely accused of being sex workers (Nadal et al., 2012), demonstrating that these biases and microaggressions could even have legal implications.

4) Discomfort or disapproval of LGBTQ experience:

These types of microaggressions include instances when LGBTQ people are treated with awkwardness, condemnation, or both. This takes place any time a couple looks at my fiancée and me in disgust as we hold hands in public. It also occurs when people proclaim that my sexual orientation is "an abomination" or that a transgender person's gender identity is "unnatural." One recent example of this in the media is the story of a transgender scientist who was outed and ridiculed for her gender identity by a journalist. While the article was supposed to focus on one of her inventions, the writer chose to instead focus the article on her gender identity. While instances like this may occur for many LGBTQ people, this story is especially tragic because the transgender woman who was targeted eventually committed suicide.

5) Assumption of sexual pathology or abnormality:

These microaggressions come about when heterosexual people consider LGBTQ people to be sexual deviants or overly sexual. One example of this on a systemic level is the federal ban for any man who has had sex with another man to donate blood. So even if a man is HIV-negative and has been in a monogamous relationship all of his life, he is considered to be at risk and therefore an ineligible donor. In the media, an example includes one time when Paris Hilton said that gay men are "disgusting" and "probably have AIDS" or recently when *The Bachelor* said that gay people were "more 'pervert' in a sense.'" In everyday life, a common occurrence is when people assume that LGBTQ people would be child molesters and are wary about LGBTQ teachers or babysitters. Anytime that any straight man assumes that I would hit on them, not only are they mistakenly flattering themselves, they are communicating that they think that all gay men can't keep their hands to themselves.

6) Denial of bodily privacy:

These kinds of microaggressions occur toward transgender people primarily and include interactions in which others feel entitled or comfortable to objectify transgender bodies. For instance, when Katie Couric recently asked Carmen Carrera about her genitals, she inappropriately and invasively asked a question that would never been asked toward a cisgender person (i.e., a person whose gender identity matches their birth sex). How would you feel if someone asked you about your genitalia on national television?

Why does this matter?

All of these microaggressions have a significant impact on people's lives. While some of these experiences may seem brief and harmless, **many studies have found that the more that people experience microaggressions, the more likely they are to report symptoms of depression, psychological distress, and even physical health issues**. For instance, I recently published a study that found that the more racial microaggressions that people of color experience, the more likely they are to also report depressive symptoms and a negative view of the world (Nadal et al., 2014). In another study, LGBTQ participants described that when they experienced microaggressions, they felt depressed, anxious, and even traumatized (Nadal, Wong, et al., 2011). Furthermore, given that LGBTQ youth are known to have a higher prevalence of substance abuse, homelessness, and suicide (see Nadal, 2013 for a review), it is even more important for us to try to minimize microaggressions and make the world a better place for them.

So what can you do?

Well, first of all, let's get everyone to stop saying things like "That's so gay!" or "That's so queer!" If something is weird, say it's "weird"! Why do you have to bring LGBTQ people into it? Correct others when they use homophobic/ transphobic language or endorse LGBTQ stereotypes. Let's teach our kids to love people, instead of hating them. We have the power to transform this next generation of young people to be open-minded and awesome. Let's do this together.

Second, let's admit when we commit microaggressions, learn from the wrongdoing, and apologize. We all make mistakes, consciously and not, and we need to own up to them when we do. Listen to what they are trying to tell you and try not to be defensive.

The worst thing that we can do is to deny that someone is hurt or offended by something we said or did; in fact, invalidating their experience could be considered a microaggression itself.

For example, when Piers Morgan interviewed transgender author Janet Mock on his show this past week, an onscreen description of Ms. Mock read "was a boy until age 18." Meanwhile, during the show, his Twitter account read: "How would you feel if you found out the woman you are dating was formerly a man?" Ms. Mock, along with many transgender supporters and cisgender allies, replied to Mr. Morgan via Twitter, calling him out on his bias. Instead of recognizing that he may have offended people, Mr. Morgan reacted with tweets like:

> Piers Morgan @piersmorgan
> Very disappointed in @janetmock's tweets tonight.
> Deliberately, and falsely, fueling some sense of me
> being 'transphobic'. Unpleasant. 1:15 AM - Feb 5, 2014

> Piers Morgan @piersmorgan
> As for all the enraged transgender supporters, look
> at how STUPID you're being. I'm on your side, you
> dimwits. @janetmock 2:16 AM - Feb 5, 2014

While I don't believe that Mr. Morgan was intentionally trying to be hurtful (in fact, he likely views himself as a transgender ally), his focus on Ms. Mock's birth sex and the sensationalizing of her transition is a common microaggression that transgender people experience. Perhaps if he could fully empathize with transgender people and the dehumanization they experience daily, he would have not gotten so defensive. In fact, he might have been able to apologize and have demonstrated a true teachable moment.

And, finally, for my LGBTQ brothers and sisters, I leave you with a couple of things. First, the next time you experience a microaggression, know that you are not alone. Sadly, these are common experiences of our lives, but I hope you find some comfort in knowing there are millions of people who can relate to you. Second, let's try not to commit microaggressions against each other either. Our community has been through a lot and we really need to work together.

References:

Gay, Lesbian and Straight Education Network (2010). *The 2009 National School Climate Survey: The Experiences of Lesbian, Gay, Bisexual and Transgender Youth in our Nation's Schools.* New York: GLSEN.

Nadal, K. L. (2013). *That's So Gay! Microaggressions and the Lesbian, Gay, Bisexual, and Transgender Community.* Washington DC: American Psychological Association.

Nadal, K. L., Griffin, K. E., Wong, Y., Hamit, S., & Rasmus, M. (2014). Racial microaggressions and mental health: Counseling clients of color. *Journal of Counseling and Development. 92*(1), 57-66.

Nadal, K. L. Issa, M., Leon, J., Meterko, V., Wideman, M., & Wong, Y. (2011). Sexual orientation microaggressions: "Death by a thousand cuts" for lesbian, gay, and bisexual youth. *Journal of LGBT Youth, 8*(3), 1-26.

Nadal, K. L., Rivera, D. P., & Corpus, M. J. H. (2010) Sexual orientation and transgender microaggressions in everyday life: Experiences of lesbians, gays, bisexuals, and transgender individuals. In D. W. Sue (Ed.), *Microaggressions and Marginality: Manifestation, Dynamics, and Impact* (pp. 217-240). New York: Wiley.

Nadal, K. L., Skolnik, A., & Wong, Y. (2012). Interpersonal and systemic microaggressions: Psychological impacts on transgender individuals and communities. *Journal of LGBT Issues in Counseling, 6*(1), 55-82.

Nadal, K. L., Wong, Y., Issa, M., Meterko, V., Leon, J., & Wideman, M. (2011). Sexual orientation microaggressions: Processes and coping mechanisms for lesbian, gay, and bisexual individuals. *Journal of LGBT Issues in Counseling, 5*(1), 21-46.

Sue, D. W., Capodilupo, C. M., Torino, G. C., Bucceri, J. M., Holder, A. M., Nadal, K. L., & Esquilin, M. E. (2007). Racial microaggressions in everyday life: Implications for counseling. *The American Psychologist, 62*(4), 271-286.

Subtle Racial Microaggressions
Can Be the Most Toxic

Tori DeAngelis

Tori DeAngelis is a freelance writer from Syracuse, New York, who has written articles covering psychology, health, medicine, culture, spirituality and other topics. Her work has appeared in outlets like the New York Times, Psychology Today, *the* Washingtonian, Common Boundary, *and* Environmental Health Perspectives.

Two colleagues—one Asian-American, the other African-American—board a small plane. A flight attendant tells them they can sit anywhere, so they choose seats near the front of the plane and across the aisle from each another so they can talk.

At the last minute, three white men enter the plane and take the seats in front of them. Just before takeoff, the flight attendant, who is white, asks the two colleagues if they would mind moving to the back of the plane to better balance the plane's load. Both react with anger, sharing the same sense that they are being singled out to symbolically "sit at the back of the bus." When they express these feelings to the attendant, she indignantly denies the charge, saying she was merely trying to ensure the flight's safety and give the two some privacy.

Were the colleagues being overly sensitive, or was the flight attendant being racist?

For Teachers College, Columbia University psychologist Derald Wing Sue, PhD—the Asian-American colleague on the plane, incidentally—the onus falls on the flight attendant. In his view, she was guilty of a "racial microaggression"—one of the "everyday insults, indignities and demeaning messages sent to people of color by well-intentioned white people who are unaware of the hidden messages being sent to them," in Sue's definition.

In other words, she was acting with bias—she just didn't know it, he says.

Sue and his team are developing a theory and classification system to describe and measure the phenomenon to help people of color understand what is going on and perhaps to educate white people as well, Sue says.

"It's a monumental task to get white people to realize that they are delivering microaggressions, because it's scary to them," he contends. "It assails their self-image of being good, moral, decent human beings to realize that maybe at an unconscious level they have biased thoughts, attitudes and feelings that harm people of color."

To better understand the type and range of these incidents, Sue and other researchers are also exploring the concept among specific groups and documenting how a regular dose of these psychological slings and arrows may erode people's mental health, job performance and the quality of social experience.

Aversive racism

The term racial microaggressions was first proposed by psychiatrist Chester M. Pierce, MD, in the 1970s, but psychologists have significantly amplified the concept in recent years.

In his landmark work on stereotype threat, for instance, Stanford University psychology professor Claude Steele, PhD, has shown that African-Americans and women perform worse on academic tests when primed with stereotypes about race or gender. Women who were primed with stereotypes about women's poor math performance do worse on math tests. Blacks' intelligence test scores plunge when they're primed with stereotypes about blacks' inferior intelligence.

Meanwhile, social psychologists Jack Dovidio, PhD, of Yale University, and Samuel L. Gaertner, PhD, of the University of Delaware, have demonstrated across several studies that many well-intentioned whites who consciously believe in and profess equality unconsciously act in a racist manner, particularly in ambiguous circumstances. In experimental job interviews, for example, whites tend not to discriminate against black candidates when their qualifications are as strong or as weak as whites'. But when candidates' qualifications are similarly ambiguous, whites tend to favor white over black candidates, the team has found. The team calls this pattern "aversive racism," referring in part to whites' aversion to being seen as prejudiced, given their conscious adherence to egalitarian principles.

Sue adds to these findings by naming, detailing and classifying the actual manifestations of aversive racism. His work illuminates the internal experiences of people affected by microaggressions—a new direction, since past research on prejudice and discrimination has focused on whites' attitudes and behaviors, notes Dovidio.

"The study of microaggressions looks at the impact of these subtle racial expressions from the perspective of the people being victimized, so it adds to our psychological understanding of the whole process of stigmatization and bias," Dovidio says.

Research shows that uncertainty is very distressing to people, Dovidio adds. "It's the uncertainty of microaggressions that can have such a tremendous impact on people of color," including on the job, in academic performance and even in therapy, he and others find.

Creating a vocabulary

Sue first proposed a classification of racial microaggressions in a 2007 article on how they manifest in clinical practice in the *American Psychologist* (Vol. 2, No. 4). There, he notes three types of current racial transgressions:

Microassaults: Conscious and intentional actions or slurs, such as using racial epithets, displaying swastikas or deliberately serving a white person before a person of color in a restaurant.

Microinsults: Verbal and nonverbal communications that subtly convey rudeness and insensitivity and demean a person's racial heritage or identity. An example is an employee who asks a colleague of color how she got her job, implying she may have landed it through an affirmative action or quota system.

Microinvalidations: Communications that subtly exclude, negate or nullify the thoughts, feelings or experiential reality of a person of color. For instance, white people often ask Asian-Americans where they were born, conveying the message that they are perpetual foreigners in their own land.

Sue focuses on microinsults and microinvalidiations because of their less obvious nature, which puts people of color in a psychological bind, he asserts: While the person may feel insulted, she is not sure exactly why, and the perpetrator doesn't acknowledge that anything has happened because he is not aware he has been offensive.

"The person of color is caught in a Catch-22: If she confronts the perpetrator, the perpetrator will deny it," Sue says.

In turn, that leaves the person of color to question what actually happened. The result is confusion, anger and an overall sapping of energy, he says.

Refining the concept

While Sue's 2007 *American Psychologist* article mainly laid out his theory and an initial taxonomy of microaggressions, his team is now examining how these subtle communications vary among different populations. In a qualitative study in the June *Professional Psychology: Research and Practice* (Vol. 39, No. 3), Sue and his colleagues conducted focus groups with 13 African-Americans who discussed their perceptions of, reactions to and interpretations of microaggressions, as well as the emotional toll they take. Participants, age 22 to 32, all lived in the New York metropolitan area and were either graduate students or worked in higher education.

Respondents agreed that these backhanded communications can make them feel as if they don't belong, that they are abnormal or that they are untrustworthy. Some described the terrible feeling of being watched suspiciously in stores as if they were about to steal something, for instance. Some reported anticipating the impact of their race by acting preemptively: One man noted how he deliberately relaxes his body while in close quarters with white women so he doesn't frighten them.

Others cited the pressure to represent their group in a positive way. One woman said she was constantly vigilant about her work performance because she was worried that any slipups would negatively affect every black person who came after her.

A similar study in the January 2007 *Cultural Diversity and Ethnic Minority Psychology* (Vol. 13, No. 1) found that many Asian-Americans cited the experience of people asking them where they were born or telling them they "spoke good English," which gave them the message that they are "aliens." Others described classroom experiences where teachers or students assumed they were great in math, which led to feelings of being trapped in a stereotype that wasn't necessarily true. Female participants complained that white men interested in dating them assumed they would be subservient sexual partners who would take care of their every need.

"These incidents may appear small, banal and trivial, but we're beginning to find they assail the mental health of recipients," Sue says.

Other researchers are showing the harm of racial microaggressions in a variety of arenas, though research in the area is still sparse, Sue acknowledges. For instance, in a 2007 article in *American Behavioral Scientist* (Vol. 51, No. 4), University of Utah social psychologist William A. Smith, PhD, and colleagues conducted focus groups with 36 black male students on five elite campuses, including Harvard and the University of Michigan.

Participants reported experiencing racial microaggressions in academic, social and public settings. For instance, some participants reported that when they went to their school's computer lab to do schoolwork, white students would call security to make sure they weren't there to cause trouble. When security arrived, they would check the students' IDs, sometimes asking them to provide a second one to prove the first was valid.

In another case, fraternity students who had gathered for practice found themselves surrounded by police vehicles, the result of someone calling in a concern about gang activity, Smith notes.

Meanwhile, in therapy, the more likely black people are to perceive their therapist using racial microaggressions, the weaker the therapeutic bond and the lower their reported satisfaction, finds a 2007 study in the *Journal of Counseling Psychology* (Vol. 54, No. 1). Sue and other researchers are beginning to study the impact of racial microaggressions on other groups as well, including people of various ethnic groups, people with disabilities, and gay, lesbian, bisexual and transgendered individuals.

Mountain or mole hill?

Not everyone agrees that microaggressions are as rampant or destructive as Sue says they are. In rebuttal letters to the 2007 *American Psychologist* article, respondents accuse Sue of blowing the phenomenon out of proportion and advancing an unnecessarily negative agenda.

"Implementing his theory would restrict rather than promote candid interaction between members of different racial groups," maintains Kenneth R. Thomas, PhD, of the University of Wisconsin–Madison, one of the critics. In the therapy relationship, for example, having to watch every word "potentially discourages therapist genuineness and spontaneity," says Thomas, who is white.

Likewise, aspects of Sue's theory enforce a victim mentality by creating problems where none exist, Thomas asserts. "The theory, in general, characterizes people of color as weak and vulnerable, and reinforces a culture of victimization instead of a culture of opportunity," he says.

Kenneth Sole, PhD, whose consulting firm Sole & Associates Inc., trains employees on team communication, agrees with Sue that microaggressions are pervasive and potentially damaging. Indeed, clients talk about them all of the time, he says. But instead of encouraging their anger, he works with them on ways to frame the incidents so they feel empowered rather than victimized, he notes.

"My own view is that we don't serve ourselves well in the hundreds of ambiguous situations we experience by latching onto the definition of the experience that gives us the greatest pain"—particularly in one-time encounters where one can't take more systemic action, he says.

For instance, if a white person makes a potentially offensive remark to a person of color, the person could choose either to get angry and see the person as a bigot or to perceive the person as ignorant and move on, he says.

For Sue's part, he believes it's important to keep shining a light on the harm these encounters can inflict, no matter how the person of color decides to handle a given encounter.

"My hope is to make the invisible visible," he says. "Microaggressions hold their power because they are invisible, and therefore they don't allow us to see that our actions and attitudes may be discriminatory."

Microaggressions Have a Damaging Effect on Therapy Patients

Nathaniel Granger

Nathaniel Granger is an adjunct faculty member at Saybrook University in Oakland, California. His doctoral dissertation was entitled "Perceptions of Racial Microaggressions among African American Males in Higher Education: A Heuristic Inquiry."

Racial, gender, sexual orientation, and other microaggressions have an unspoken and damaging effect on the therapeutic process.

Solórzano, Ceja, & Yosso, (as cited in Granger, 2011), define microaggressions as brief, everyday exchanges that send denigrating messages to certain individuals because of their group membership (people of color, women, lesbian, gay, bisexual, or transgender (LGBTs)). The term was first coined by Pierce in 1970 in his work with Black Americans where he defined it as "subtle, stunning, often automatic, and nonverbal exchanges which are 'put-downs'" (Pierce, Carew, Pierce-Gonzalez, & Willis, 1978, p. 66). They have also been described as "subtle insults (verbal, nonverbal, and/or visual) directed toward people of color, often automatically or unconsciously."

Sue expounded on the definition as noted: Brief and commonplace daily verbal, behavioral, and environmental indignities, whether intentional or unintentional, that communicate hostile, derogatory, or negative racial, gender, sexual orientation, and religious slights and insults to the target person or group, (Sue, 2010). Sue's research related to the psychology of microaggressions indicates that White individuals are often unaware of the cumulative harm that people of color experience from being routinely subjected to various racial microaggressions.

"Microaggressions and Their Effects on the Therapeutic Process," by Nathaniel Granger, Society for Humanistic Psychology, October 2012. Reprinted by Permission.

Bonilla-Silva (as cited in Granger, 2011) defined subtle forms of racial bias, referred to as *color-blind racism* refer to the conception among White individuals that considerations of race are presently no longer relevant in people's lives in the United States. Contemporary color-blind racism is expressed in everyday beliefs, attitudes, and behaviors that are considered acceptable, and even commendable, by White individuals who use them. Accordingly, such attitudes are so deeply embedded in societal values and practices that they lie outside the consciousness of many well-intentioned White people who may genuinely consider themselves to be nonracist (Sue, 2003).

According to Sue, *microinvalidations,* a type of microaggression, are characterized by communications or environmental cues that exclude, negate, or nullify the psychological thoughts, feelings, or experiential reality of certain groups, such as people of color, women, and LGBTs. In many ways, microinvalidations may potentially represent the most damaging form of microaggressions because they directly and insidiously deny the racial, gender, or sexual-orientation reality of these groups. According to Sue, the power to impose reality upon marginalized groups represents the ultimate form of oppression (Sue, 2010). Examples of microinvalidations can be heard in everyday statements such as *low man on the totem pole.*

The therapeutic relationship

The establishment of rapport is paramount to good therapy. In helping professions, this is referred to as the "therapeutic working alliance," and most professionals agree that a successful outcome is related to the quality, nature, and strength of the therapeutic relationship. On a dynamic level, counseling and psychotherapy may be defined as a process of interpersonal interaction, communication, and influence between helping professionals and their clients. For effective therapy to occur, several conditions must be part of the process:

- Communication must be clear, accurate, and appropriate,
- The helping professional must establish credibility in the eyes of the client.

When microaggressions are unknowingly and inappropriately delivered by the helping professional, communication clarity and credibility suffer with the possibility of creating a rupture or impasse in the helping relationship.

When critical consciousness and awareness is lacking, when one is fearful about clarifying the meaning of tension-filled interactions, and when one actively avoids pursuing an understanding of these dynamics, the offenses remain invisible (Goodman, 1995). Indeed, avoidance of race topics has been likened to "a conspiracy of silence". According to Sue, (as cited in Granger, 2011), making the *invisible* visible is the first step toward combating unconscious and unintentional racism, sexism, heterosexism, and other forms of bigotry festering under the sheath of microaggressions.

Examples of racial, gender and sexual orientation microaggressions in therapeutic practice

- Aliens in One's Own Land
- Ascription of Intelligence
- Color Blindness
- Criminality/Assumption of Criminal Status
- Use of Sexist/Heterosexist Language
- Denial of Individual Racism/Sexism/Heterosexism
- Myth of Meritocracy
- Pathologizing Cultural Values/Communication Styles
- Second-Class Citizen
- Culturally Insensitive/Antagonistic Treatment
- Traditional Gender Role Prejudicing and Stereotyping
- Sexual Objectification
- Assumption of Abnormality

The way forward

Four objectives can be distilled from the definition that has relevance to combatting microaggressions:

- Making the "invisible" visible
- Establishing expertise and trust
- Providing appropriate services to diverse populations
- The old adage "physician [therapist], heal thyself" before healing others is all-important in having helping professionals become aware of their values, biases, and assumptions about human behavior.

Acquiring knowledge and understanding of the worldviews of diverse groups and clients are all important in providing culturally relevant services. Helping professionals must begin the process of developing culturally appropriate and effective intervention strategies in working with clients different from them. Additionally, helping professionals must develop skills that involve interventions aimed at organizational structures, policies, practices, and regulations within institutions, if they are to become culturally competent.

Principles to employ to lessen the effects of microaggressions in therapy

- Principle One—Learn about people of color, women and LGBTs from sources within the group.
- Principle Two—Learn from healthy and strong people of the group.
- Principle Three—Learn from experiential reality.
- Principle Four—Learn from constant vigilance of biases and fears.
- Principle Five—Learn by being committed to personal action against racism, sexism and heterosexism.

As long as microaggressions remain hidden, invisible, unspoken and excused as innocent slights with minimal harm, individuals will continue to insult, demean, alienate, and oppress marginalized groups. In the realm of racial microaggressions, for example, studies indicate that racial microaggressions are often triggers to difficult dialogues on race in the classroom and the clinical setting, as well. Clients and therapists are confused and uncertain about what is transpiring, and both, therapists and clients are very "hung up" on clarifying these racial interactions for fear of appearing racist. It behooves professionals as well as laypersons alike to recognize and make every effort to ameliorate the effects of microaggression on the therapeutic process.

References

Boykin, A.W., Jagers, R.J., Ellison, C.M., & Albury, A. (1997). Communalism: Conceptualization and measurement of an afrocultural social orientation. *Journal of Black Studies, 27*(3), 409-418. doi: 10.1177/002193479702700308

Boykin, A.W., & Toms, F.D. (1985). Black child socialization: A cultural framework. In H.P. McAdoo & J.L. McAdoo (Eds.), *Black children: Social, educational, and parental environments* (pp. 33-51). Newbury Park, CA: Sage.

Goodman, D. J. (1995). Difficult dialogues: Enhancing discussions about diversity. *College Teaching, 43*, 47 – 52.

Granger, N. (2011). Perceptions of racial microaggressions among African American males in higher education: A heuristic inquiry.

Sue, D.W. (2010). *Microaggressions in everyday life: Race, gender, and sexual orientation.* Hoboken, NJ: Wiley.

Triandis, H.C., Chan, D.K.S., Bhawuk, D.P.S., Iwao, S., & Sinha, J.B.P. (1995). Multimethod probes of allocentrism and idiocentrism. *International Journal of Psychology, 30*(4), 461- 480.

The Jury's Still Out on What Constitutes a Microaggression

Musa Al-Gharbi

Musa Al-Gharbi is the Paul F. Lazarsfeld Fellow in Sociology at Columbia University and a research associate at Heterodox Academy. His focus includes social psychology, semiotics, cognitive sociology, and applied social epistemology.

The concept of microaggressions gained prominence with the publication of Sue et al.'s 2007, "Racial Microaggressions in Everyday Life," which defined microaggressions as communicative, somatic, environmental or relational cues that demean and/or disempower members of minority groups in virtue of their minority status.[1] Microaggressions, they asserted, are typically subtle and ambiguous. Often, they are inadvertent or altogether unconscious. For these reasons, they are also far more pervasive than other, more overt, forms of bigotry (which are less-tolerated in contemporary America). The authors propose a tripartite taxonomy of microaggressions:

- *Microassaults* involve explicit and intentional racial derogation;
- *Microinsults* involve rudeness or insensitivity towards another's heritage or identity;
- *Microinvalidations* occur when the thoughts and feelings of a minority group member seem to be excluded, negated or nullified as a result of their minority status.

The authors go on to present anecdotal evidence suggesting that repeated exposure to microaggressions is detrimental to the well-being of minorities. Moreover, they assert, a lack of awareness about the prevalence and impact of microaggressions among mental health professionals could undermine the practice

Musa Al-Gharbi. Originally published as "Microaggressions, Macro Debate." Heterodox Academy, January 30, 2017. Reprinted by permission.

of clinical psychology—reducing the quality and accessibility of care for those who may need it most.

Towards the conclusion, however, the authors acknowledge the "nascent" state of research on microaggressions and call for further investigation. They emphasize that future studies should focus first and foremost on *empirically substantiating the harm caused by microaggressions, and documenting how people cope (or fail to cope) with experiencing them.* They suggest further research should also probe whether or not there is systematic variation as to who incurs microaggressions, which type or types of microaggressions particular populations tend to endure, how harmful microaggressions are to different groups, and in which contexts microaggressions tend to be more (or less) prevalent or harmful. Finally, the authors recommend expanding microaggression research to include incidents against gender and sexual minorities, and those with disabilities.

The State of Microaggression Research Today

In the decade following Sue et al.'s landmark paper, there have been extensive discussions about microaggressions—among practitioners, in the academic literature, and increasingly, in popular media outlets and public forums. But unfortunately, very little empirical research has been conducted to actually substantiate the ubiquity of microaggressions, to catalog the harm they cause, or to refine the authors' initial taxonomy.

In "Microaggressions: Strong Claims, Inadequate Evidence," Scott Lilienfeld highlights five core premises undergirding the microaggression research program (MRP):[2]

- Microaggressions are operationalized with sufficient clarity and consensus to afford rigorous scientific investigation.
- Microaggressions are interpreted negatively by most or all minority group members.
- Microaggressions reflect implicitly prejudicial and implicitly aggressive motives.

- Microaggressions can be validly assessed using only respondents' subjective reports.
- Microaggressions exert an adverse impact on recipient's mental health.

His comprehensive meta-analysis suggests that there is "negligible" support for these axioms—individually or (especially) collectively.

However, Lilienfeld emphasizes that an absence of evidence regarding the prevalence and harm of microaggressions should *not* be interpreted as evidence of absence. Over the course of the essay he repeatedly asserts that it is "undeniable" that minorities regularly experience slights which could be construed as microaggressions; he acknowledges that these incidents are often deeply unpleasant or unsettling for affected minorities, and likely harmful in aggregate. Nonetheless, important research questions remain, namely: *how* harmful are microaggressions, for *whom, in what ways* and *under what circumstances*?

These are not just a matters of intellectual curiosity, but instead, prerequisites for crafting effective responses, evaluating attempted interventions, and minimizing iatrogenesis[3] along the way. It is similarly critical to clarify and substantiate claims about microaggressions for the sake of blunting skepticism and resistance—particularly from those whose identity, perceived interests and routines are most likely to be challenged by reforms in social norms, practices and policies (i.e. those who are white, native-born, heterosexual, able in body and mind, economically-comfortable and/or men). Finally, it is essential to the continued integrity and credibility of social research that basic evidentiary standards be met—especially for strong psychological claims—particularly in light of how prominent and politicized the issue of microaggressions has become. In other words, it is in *everyone's* interest to address the profound conceptual and evidentiary shortcomings of the MRP literature to date.

Evidentiary Gaps

According to Lilienfeld, one of the most striking aspects of microaggression research is that over the course of nearly ten years, the literature has hardly advanced beyond the taxonomy and methods laid out in the original paper.

For instance, with regards to demonstrating the harm caused by microaggressions, there has been very little engagement with contemporary cognitive or behavioral research—and virtually no experimental testing. Instead, advocates have relied almost exclusively on small collections of anecdotal testimonies, from samples that are neither randomized nor established as representative of any particular population. This is problematic, Lilienfeld asserts, because the preponderance of contemporary social psychological research strongly suggests that the perception of, and response to, microaggressions would vary a great deal between and within minority populations as a result of individuals' particular situational, cognitive, psychological, cultural, and personality traits.[4]

It is important to account for these factors in order to isolate and better measure the potential harm caused by microaggressions. Identifying the impact of particular traits on microaggression response could also help researchers determine who is most sensitive to perceiving microaggressions, and who is most adversely affected by them—allowing for tailored interventions to better assist those who are particularly vulnerable. Meanwhile, collecting information on the base-rates of microaggressions can help researchers identify exemplary environments where these incidents seem relatively rare, as well as environments which seem especially toxic. This can help prioritize interventions and provide models for reform. Base-rate information is also essential for evaluating whether particular interventions seem to be increasing, decreasing or failing to impact the prevalence of microaggressions…not to mention determining how bad the problem is to begin with.

Conceptual Problems

Beyond the evidentiary gaps, Lilienfeld asserts that one of the biggest problems with microaggression literature is the lack of clarity on exactly what *constitutes* a microaggression, what *does not*, and *in virtue of what*. As things currently stand, the microaggression concept is so inclusive that even those committed to doing the "right thing" often find themselves in impossible situations. Consider the following example:

A white teacher puts forward a question the class. A number of students raise their hands to answer—including some minority students. According to the literature, if the teacher fails to call on the minority student(s), this could be interpreted as a microaggression by favoring the dominant perspectives at the expense of minorities. However, deciding to call on a minority student would merely create a new dilemma: if the instructor criticizes or challenges any aspect of the student's response, this could be construed as a microaggression as well: invalidating their perspective. On the other hand, if the teacher praises the student's answer as insightful or articulate, this might *also* be considered a microaggression: why should it be remarkable or noteworthy that the minority student provided an apt response?

That is, for those who are "privileged" (i.e. white, native-born, heterosexual, able in body and mind, economically-comfortable and/or a man), virtually anything one says or does could be construed as a microaggression.[5] In such a climate it may seem desirable or even necessary for many to minimize interactions with those outside their identity group(s) in order to avoid needless (but otherwise seemingly inevitable) conflict.[6] This is a major problem given that, according to Sue et al., the main purpose of the MRP is to foster broader and deeper openness, understanding, dialogue and cooperation.

Lillenfeld suggests that the term "microaggression" causes further polarization: "Aggression" implies hostile intent. Yet microaggressions, as defined in the literature, tend to involve neither hostility nor intent. Most violations are microinsults and microinvalidations—which are typically unintentional slights resulting from ignorance, insensitivity or unconscious bias among people of good-will. By classifying such incidents as "microaggressions," those who commit these *faux pas* as "perpetrators," and those who experience them as "victims" all parties involved become disposed towards responding to incidents in a confrontational rather than conciliatory fashion,[7] as both sides feel unfairly maligned or mistreated.

Lilienfeld suggests advocates would be better served by revising terms and concepts to better capture the indirect and typically inadvertent nature of the phenomena in question. Microassaults, he argues, should probably be struck from the taxonomy altogether: the examples provided in the literature tend not to be "micro" at all, but outright assaults, intimidation, harassment and bigotry–even rising to the level of crimes in some instances. In contrast with microinvalidations or microinsults, microassaults are necessarily overt, intentional and hateful acts. Including these types of incidents as "microaggressions" is both unnecessary and confusing.

Derald Wing Sue Responds

In "Racial Microaggressions in Everyday Life" Sue and his collaborators acknowledged the need for further empirical research on microaggressions, and suggested avenues future work should prioritize. Lilienfeld has argued that these recommendations have gone largely unheeded, and as a result, many of the authors' claims remain just as tenuous in 2017 as they were in 2007. In a rejoinder,[8] entitled "Microaggressions and 'Evidence': Empirical or Experiential Reality?" Sue declines to contest Lilienfeld's overall picture. In fact, he acknowledges that the critiques are generally valid—adding that he actually shares many of the concerns Lilienfeld raised about the contemporary state of microaggression research.

Given this apparently broad agreement between Sue and Lilienfeld, most of the rest of the rejoinder proves perplexing. For instance, despite having called for further empirical research on multiple occasions himself, Sue claims (without support) that highlighting conceptual or evidentiary gaps in the MRP somehow undermines or negates the phenomenological significance of microaggressions. This assertion is particularly baffling given that Lilienfeld repeatedly calls for *greater* emphasis and attention to the subjective reality of microaggressions in the paper Sue is responding to.

More confusing is Dr. Sue's insinuation that it may not be necessary to experimentally validate microaggressions at all: psychology, science and empiricism are not the only ways of understanding human experience, nor are they necessarily the best method(s) in every instance. Of course, one anticipates Lilienfeld would simply agree with this point—albeit while insisting that context also matters with regards to which tools or frameworks are most useful or important.

In the 2007 essay and subsequent works, Dr. Sue was speaking *as a psychologist*, and relying on his credentials *as a psychologist* to publish and disseminate his work—often in journals related to the social and behavioral sciences or the clinical practice of psychology /psychiatry. Engaging in these capacities entails agreeing to the evidentiary, methodological and ethical norms or standards of one's chosen profession or field. Lilienfeld was arguing that the current state of research on microaggressions seems to fall short in these regards—nothing more, nothing less. So there is a sense in which Sue's response, evoking questions about the ultimate nature of truth or humanity, is more-or-less irrelevant to Lilienfeld's claims. It also seems deeply problematic for Sue to put forward microaggression research *as scientific* when this seems to lend credibility to his project, but then claim microaggressions need not be subject to empirical testing when faced with criticism.

Ultimately, Sue responds directly to only one of Lilienfeld's 18 recommendations—namely that until microaggressions are better understood, we should be conservative in executing policies intended to address them. Sue condescendingly dismisses this suggestion, asserting that only "[t]hose in the majority group, those with power and privilege, and those who do not experience microaggressions are privileged to enjoy the luxury of waiting for proof."

Such a reply is striking given the long and ignoble history of harm caused by hastily applied (and often later discredited) social and psychological research—with the costs borne primarily by women, people of color, the poor and other vulnerable populations.[9] In other words, Lilienfeld's advice should not be understood as an expression of privilege: guarding against *iatrogenesis* and adverse second order effects is important, including for minorities—in fact, on average these safeguards prove *especially* critical for minorities given their already more precarious socio-economic position. In this instance, it seems highly plausible that poorly conceived or implemented policies intended to address microaggressions could endanger the free exchange of ideas, lead to unjustly severe consequences for minor (even unintentional) infractions, heighten animus between minority and majority groups, or even *exacerbate* the harm caused by microaggressions (for instance by making already-vulnerable individuals even more sensitive to perceived slights or injustices).[10] In virtually any of these eventualities everyone—including minorities—may be worse off than before. This possibility seems to warrant more than a snarky retort about Lilienfeld's supposed privilege.

More reliable data on the prevalence and harm of microaggressions could help to avoid these negative externalities by enabling more nuanced policy responses from university administrators. Sue was correct in calling for this research in 2007, and Lillenfeld is correct in reaffirming that call ten years later.

Notes

1. Sue, Derald et al. (2007). "Racial Microaggressions in Everyday Life: Implications for Clinical Practice." *American Psychologist* 62(4): 271-86.

2. Lillenfeld, Scott (2017). "Microaggressions: Strong Claims, Inadequate Evidence." *Perspectives on Psychological Science* 12(1): 138-69.

3. For an accessible introduction to the concept of iatrogenesis as it relates to these issues see: Ghraiba, Noomen (2006). "Adverse Effects and Iatrogenesis in Psychotherapy." *Psychotherapy in the Arab World* 9: 69-71.

4. For a good summary on the variable impacts of negative emotions on mental health, see: Rodriguez, Tori (2013). "Negative Emotions Are Key to Well-Being." *Scientific American,* 1 May.

5. Campbell, Bradley & Jason Manning (2014). "Microaggressions and Moral Cultures." *Comparative Sociology 13(6):* 692-726.

6. For an examples of this mentality see: Dreher, Rod (2017). "The Left, Feeding the Alt-Right." *The American Conservative,* 13 August.

7. For elaboration on this point see: Haidt, Jonathan & Greg Lukianoff (2017). "Why It's a Really Bad Idea to Tell Students Words Are Violence." *The Atlantic,* 18 July.

8. Sue, Derald (2017). "Microaggressions and 'Evidence': Empirical or Experiential Reality?" *Perspectives on Psychological Science* 12(1): 170-2.

9. For more on this point see: Easterly, William (2015). *The Tyranny of Experts: Economists, Dictators and the Forgotten Rights of the Poor.* New York, NY: Basic Books. Leonard, Thomas (2016). *Illiberal Reformers: Race, Eugenics, and American Economics in the Progressive Era.* Princeton, NJ: Princeton University Press.

10. For more on these points: al-Gharbi, Musa (2017). "A Lack of Ideological Diversity is Killing Social Research." *Times Higher Education,* 23 March. ibid. (2015). "White People Are Not the Enemy." *Salon,* August 25. Lukianoff, Greg (2014). *Unlearning Liberty: Campus Censorship and the End of American Debate.* New York, NY: Encounter Books. Taleb, Nassim (2014). "Naïve Intervention." *Antifragile: Things That Gain from Disorder.* New York, NY: Random House. pp. 110-33.

The Term "Microaggression" Should Be Retired Until It Is Better Understood

Bobby Hristova

Toronto-based journalist Bobby Hristova is a staff writer for The Blank Page and a junior editor for Mind Matters magazine.

T rigger warning: A new literature review conducted by Scott O. Lilienfeld of Emory University recommends everyone abandon the term, 'microaggressions,' which has been used to describe subtle and unintentional acts of discrimination towards marginalized individuals. The concept is deemed too undeveloped to suggest any application in reality, as shown by Lilienfield's review.

The term was conceived in 1970 by Chester Pierce, a former psychiatrist and professor at Harvard University. Though the term is aged, it has recently seen a rebirth in media and modern pop culture after complementary research was released in 2007 by Derald Wing Sue and others.

> *"Racial microaggressions are the brief and everyday slights, insults, indignities and denigrating messages* sent *to people of color by well-intentioned White people who are unaware of the hidden messages being communicated." – Derald Wing Sue*

Essentially, what some perceive to be normal questions or thoughts are actually a sign of implicit prejudice towards marginalized groups. Microaggressions have also spawned spin-off definitions, including *microinsults*, which are contemptible, covert communications towards one's identity; *microinvalidations*, subtle communications which invalidate the experiences of marginalized groups; and *microassaults,* intentional discriminatory acts.

Thus, even if you were accused of committing a microaggression, denying such would also be a microaggression (it would be

"The major problem with microaggressions," Author: Bobby Hristova; Publisher: The Blank Page. Reprinted by permission.

considered a microinvalidation). In turn, this forces some into the uncomfortable position of accepting the accusation of racism. Another weakness is the notion that a microassault is 'micro.' Preventing a child to date someone outside of their own race, or walking around with a swastika stitched on your sweater is purely racism; there is nothing subtle about it.

As Lilienfield delved into the theory, he spotted a plethora of issues, including the criticism above. He accentuates the ambiguity within the theory, explaining microaggressions are subjective and what one individual finds hostile, another may find helpful.

One key component Lilienfield mentioned was the interplay between personality, specifically negative emotionality, and the perception of microaggressions. Negative emotionality states, traits such as hostility, neuroticism, irritability, and perceived victimization are more prevalent in some, allowing specific people to be more sensitive towards microaggressions. Existing studies surrounding stereotype threat can be found to support the notion that certain individuals are more inclined to perceive threats and victimization if they strongly identify with specific groups or domains. That is, the fear of confirming stereotypes about one's group can complement the idea that some individuals are more likely to perceive microaggressions.

In the case of group identification, Steele and Aronson found some are more susceptible to stereotype threat and what they recognize to be racial insults because the group they strongly identify with is tied to omnipresent negative stereotypes. Similarly, domain identification replicated this when African American college students anticipating an intelligence test had a significant tendency to finish word fragments like 'R_C_' with the word 'RACE' instead of other common words. Even a cue as slight as the description of an intelligence test triggered this stereotype threat, because of pre-existing stereotypes surrounding African Americans and levels of intelligence. This means there may be other cues (excluding those related to groups) prevalent in society which trigger some to be more aware of these perceived prejudicial put-downs.

Moreover, stigma consciousness, a theory developed by Elizabeth Pinel from the University of Texas, maintains that some are more aware of their stigmatized status and this leads to an increased sensitivity to being judged based on one's marginalized identity. This can result in an expectation to be stereotyped, adding to the perception of microaggressions.

The research behind microaggressions also failed to withstand Lilenfield's scrutiny. He accentuated some samples within the focus groups, which included specific individuals who already endorsed the theory. Additionally, there is a lack of depth as to whether those who commit microaggressions exhibit other prejudicial tendencies. Other methods used to evaluate this, including the famous implicit association test (IAT), have failed to conclude the notion with certainty. Another gap within the research included a lack of analysis regarding the base rate, meaning the list of microaggressions could be limitless and may account for any daily experience because they cannot be compared to an average rate of microaggression. Though these were some of the main observations, there were countless other criticisms as well.

It is important to note Lilenfield does not simply critique the theory of microaggressions, he also provides suggestions. He underscores using more established and recognized areas of psychological investigation and offers a multitude of recommendations to improve the research behind the theory.

Lilienfield proposes to replace microaggression with 'perceived racial slight' until more evidence can deem otherwise. In an age where many claim everything is offensive to someone, Lilenfield's literature review of this topic is a vital reminder to be aware of how you perceive things and to think critically about whether something actually is malicious or not. Though the theory initiated many discussions about language awareness, hopefully these new findings will create further conversation around language and how it is interpreted.

Nonetheless, until the theory and research behind microaggressions receives much needed improvement, the term should be retired.

Are Safe Spaces an Effective Way to Protect Marginalized People?

Overview: Open vs. Closed Communities as Examples of Safe Spaces

Zara Rahman

Feminist researcher and writer Zara Rahman is a Fellow at Data & Society Research Institute, where she focuses on the skills and roles needed to successfully implement technology and data projects among human rights defenders and activists.

I'm a big 'open' advocate, and inclusivity and diversity are very important to me. Over the past few months, though, I've been wondering more about "closed" communities - and, I have to say that I'm seeing more and more benefits of them. Somewhat counter-intuitively, I'm finding more and more that closed communities are actually more inclusive than many open ones. Let me explain why.

Let me start with definitions, at least as I understand them. For me, an open community is:

- one where anyone can join (whether this be a mailing list, or a physical meet up group, event or conference)
- where processes and decision making happens transparently - whether this is by an elected group of representatives, or, more likely, as a group decision
- one where anyone (newcomers, and long time community members) are welcomed to speak and voice their opinion
- one where the majority of communications are made public (eg. the archives of mailing lists are made public by default)

And a closed community is:

- invitation-only
- only members of the community can access resources, see the mailing list archives, etc.

- decision-making might happen transparently to members of the group itself, but these processes are not made public

As I said earlier, inclusivity is close to my heart, and from first glance at a closed community as I've defined it here, it seems to be the opposite of that.

But what I'm seeing is that within closed communities, someone, or some event, has brought a certain group of people together for a reason. They've already been identified as being trusted individuals, with a shared interest and affinity, and, crucially, zero interest in trolling each other. Being in a closed community which has been convened by someone you know and trust is essentially being part of a safe space online or offline - and, sadly, these are somewhat rare on the internet, especially for women and marginalised communities.

In a similar vein to the line of argument that this piece takes on newsletters being a new safe space for women - invite-only mailing lists are the places where I read some of the most valuable content I interact with online. Sometimes this is through people sharing experiences that they just wouldn't feel comfortable writing about publicly; other times, it's talking about topics that would attract too much negative attention online from trolls, or asking for advice about sensitive but important topics.

I'm noticing a similar trend in the quality of conversations, debates and discussions that I'm having at different styles of offline events, too. Over the past four years, I've attended a huge range of events - 'open' festivals, unconferences, traditional conferences with panels, small and big workshops... and in all honesty, the places where I've learned the most and done the most valuable work have been the closed, invitation only events. Retreats, work sprints, or workshops with smaller groups of people have been where I've felt like I've achieved and learned the most.

That's not to say that I've not enjoyed many of the larger, open events - I've met lots of fascinating people, had great conversations, and listened to great talks. But inevitably there's a person, or multiple, who say something sexist or racist, or the person who interrupts women on stage, condescends, makes offensive assumptions about me or others... and generally reduces my enjoyment, and the enjoyment of others. Perhaps I'm naive, but this simply hasn't happened at smaller events where every single individual has been selected by someone I trust.

And the same with many open mailing lists and discussion fora- there are people that are known for trolling but who don't get removed from the community, people who are aggressive and annoying - and, essentially, people who put off the rest of us from contributing as we would otherwise like to.

Obviously though, there are ways in which these closed communities are **not** inclusive; the main one being that there's inherently a gatekeeper somewhere there. There's no denying that that is the opposite of inclusive by very definition, and it's this that I find difficult to reconcile. I will say though that many of the invite-only mailing lists have been pretty flexible to letting people in upon recommendation from other trusted members, or from people who others have interacted with online. Similarly with the invite-only events, often a group of trusted people are asked for recommendations for others - which, though it doesn't totally remove the barrier to entry, does reduce it.

So, as a long-winded answer to my initial ponderings: which of these communities is more valuable? For me, they serve different purposes. Open communities are good for hearing from wide groups of people, sharing things that need lots of publicity (like job adverts, or notices of events), and for networking - but for valuable, intimate conversations, I actually much prefer the closed, invite-only communities and events.

I'm still unsure, though, on whether this is a good development or a bad one, though. Otherwise put, what I'm essentially saying is that I don't feel 100% comfortable at large events, or in large online discussion groups, and I have to admit that thinking that makes me sad. But until there are better-enforced codes of conduct, and more thoughtful online- and offline-behaviour of other people, I'm not sure there's any other pragmatic option.

An Argument for Safe Spaces

Anne-Laure White

Activist Anne-Laure White is a Columbia University graduate and a writer for Dissent magazine involved with several activist organizations through the Barnard Columbia Solidarity Network.

In 1981, women from all around the world—some calling themselves feminists, some driven by a call to action just as defiant but not yet named—congregated at Greenham Common in Berkshire, England to protest the decision to store ninety-six U.S. nuclear missiles there. Leaderless, the women collectively decided to oust the few men who initially joined them. They were anti-war, yes, but beyond that, they were building a vision of an ideal community, reimagining politics in which their voices were equal but distinct. Overcoming patriarchal violence not only required opposition to military nihilism, but also a positive reimagining of personal relationships, domestic tasks, and the role of government. At the time, women-only actions, like many all-black actions today, were labeled divisive. But, as Ann Snitow wrote in a 1985 essay about the occupation that appears in her new collection The Feminism of Uncertainty, "it would be unnerving indeed to most of these well-meaning men if they could glimpse how profoundly alienated many women are from men's groups and the political process." Therefore at Greenham Common, cooking and cleaning was shared, and action was decided upon by popular consensus: this community of women found themselves living a version of the peaceful egalitarianism that they were fighting for.

The feminists of Greenham Common were building on decades of activism aimed at stripping away the distinction between personal and public, the foundations of the current "safe space" debate. The term "safe space" has multiple origin stories—Moira

"The Case for Safe Spaces," by Anne-Laure White, originally published in Dissent magazine, April 25, 2016. Reprinted by permission.

Kenney's Mapping Gay L.A. links safe spaces to gay and lesbian bars, where, as Malcolm Harris described in Fusion, "a safe space meant somewhere you could be out and in good company—at least until the cops showed up" in the midst of repressive anti-sodomy laws and social discrimination. The "safe spaces" of sixties and seventies feminism offered a similar hope for good company: the hope for comrades with whom women could be equal partners in political organizing, a community in which individual women's experiences were validated not simply as either emotional or political, but as emotional and therefore political.

Young people are coming of age in a time just as ridden with inequality, and are finding a personal and political education in, or from, the safe spaces modeled by their sixties predecessors. Evan Zavidow, a facilitator for AllSex, a current Barnard/Columbia program that meets biweekly to discuss sexuality, identity, and gender, defines "safe spaces" as places that try to be inclusive, value personal safety and self care without judgment, and assume the good intent of peers. AllSex members, like the women who sought to make Greenham Common inclusive to women by asking men to leave, are attentive to how exclusion operates in ostensibly integrated environments. Alongside its mixed-gender and mixed-race sections, AllSex designates sections for specific identities based on the preferences of participants of color, women, and/or non-gender conforming people. Unlike the Greenham Common peace camp, AllSex is also attentive to language as exclusionary. The group recently changed its name from "FemSex" so as not to alienate people who did not identify as females and/or women. While AllSex is not aligned with a particular political ideology, "there is something inherently political in carving out a community of relatively diverse individuals and discussing taboo topics," says Zavidow. Similar to historic safe spaces, AllSex's biweekly sections are not necessarily engaged in public politics, but have, in Zavidow's experience, "political potential." Indeed filmmaker Beeban Kidron remembers Greenham Common as a place where women found "a voice that was predicated on inclusion and difference, multiple perspectives not a single dominant view."

Contemporary student activists recognize that their organizing must emulate their goals. Models for doing so are imperfect and perhaps intangible. In a recent Harper's forum Hannah Black pointed out that "many now use the term 'safer space' to indicate that we are talking about relative and not absolute levels of safety." But each failure to achieve safety strips away another pretense of normalcy, and raises an individual's discomfort to a communal problem. A "safe space" is neither absolute nor literal. And the outpouring of criticism against safe spaces is a testament to how challenging creating an egalitarian space can be, and how shattering to a person's sense of self.

In their widely cited Atlantic cover story, "The Coddling of the American Mind," Greg Lukianoff and Jonathan Haidt argued that while student activists of the eighties and nineties "challenged the literary, philosophical, and historical canon, seeking to widen it by including more-diverse perspectives . . . the current movement is largely about emotional well-being." But this is a false distinction. There is an emotional toll to being written out of your own history, which was put to use by activists in their struggles to change the canon. All politics are about emotional well-being. As Terrell Jermaine Starr wrote of last year's University of Missouri protests, "fueling those protests was black pain."

Lukianoff and Haidt's piece is one of a series of recent attacks on safe spaces. The black and feminist left that built safe spaces in activism is an unfortunate blind spot in the memories of leftists like Todd Gitlin, who bemoans safe spaces as evidence of "fearful" college protesters. Last November in the New York Times, Gitlin described safe spaces as evidence that "too many students doubt that their community is, or can be, strong enough to stand up for itself," comparing their seemingly useless emotions to the actions of sixties activists—"radical change is not for the narrow-minded or weak-hearted." Meanwhile each sixties-era marginalized group to which he now prescribes glory—LGBTQ activists, civil rights activists, feminists—used safe spaces as a basis for their activism. Each action that Gitlin rightfully pays homage to, from bus boycotts to organizing press, could not have happened without that blissful discovery of a community in which one, at least temporarily, feels listened to and valued equally. In painting safe spaces as illustrative of the weakness of a new generation, Gitlin ignores a fundamental component of the history in which he took part. He forgets the day before a protest: the therapeutic revelation of a common experience, the thrill of bearing your soul to a room full of comrades who validate your experiences as gendered, racial, political, and important.

An early manifestation of such safe spaces were the consciousness-raising groups of sixties feminists, which provided intimate environments for sharing personal experiences with the ultimate goal of political action. Like the safe spaces of Mizzou activists, consciousness-raising groups prioritized personal experience in making political decisions, and were often formed on the basis of shared identity and/or oppression. Barbara Epstein has described consciousness-raising groups as a means of questioning "abstract principles (so often used by men to legitimize their power)" and recognizing "personal experience and perceptions as a legitimate basis for political analysis." Activist spaces, and especially academic activist spaces, have long been dominated by the masculine preference for theory over experience. But as River Bunkley, an Emory student involved in the NAACP, Black Student Alliance, and Advocates for Racial Justice, among his many intersectional activist engagements, points out: "being able to hurt, cry, laugh, and thrive in spaces that don't seek to exploit or negate these emotions is incredibly important to the progression of my community." Emotional honesty has political significance when a community has been repeatedly silenced and dispossessed. "When people of color decide to indulge in their feelings," Bunkley told me, "there is a level of healing, unifying, and empowerment—I think—that comes with it."

Among leftists, those who have reacted most strongly against safe spaces have been white men, perhaps because grounding politics in the ability to hurt, cry, and laugh together threatens traditional notions of masculinity. Men are taught to repress emotions, associating emotional vulnerability with femininity and therefore weakness, so it is expected that some should react so violently to the idea that political discussions might take place on explicitly emotional grounds. Once emotions are given intellectual weight, how do men retain their control of political decisions? The safe space debate often appears to be a crisis of masculinity, as many criticisms are, in short, a message to students to "grow a pair."

Unlike early consciousness raising groups, contemporary models for safe spaces grapple far more with the inequalities and privileges underlying a simple conversation. Professor Shirley Geok-lin Lim, who encountered sixties consciousness-raising groups as a recent Malaysian immigrant to New York City, recalled unintentional, yet destructive and unrecognized, exclusion from groups of white feminists in her essay in The Feminist Memoir Project: "the very smallness of the consciousness-raising groups, which allowed trust to flourish, meant that large numbers of other 'non-mutual' women were not admitted . . . women of color, immigrant women, blue-collar women whose class and familial positions did not permit them the time to participate." Such exclusion continues to pervade the student left, particularly given the elite nature of institutions of higher education, but it does not remain as blatantly unchecked by students today. Columbia's anti-sexual assault group No Red Tape, for example, dwindled in popularity within activist communities despite its national recognition in spring 2015, largely due to its failure to take on an anti-racist and anti-imperialist agenda. This year, No Red Tape has returned as a force to reckon with; its members are now in solidarity and dialogue with a range of other campus activists, including Students for Justice in Palestine, Jewish Voice for Peace, Columbia Divest for Climate Justice, and Mobilized African Diaspora. Creating activist spaces in which inclusivity and collectivism are valued allows attention to individual needs and forces malleability in political demands. Bunkley describes "understanding that there are multiple ways to serve a community and multiple identities that need different things within a community" as fundamental to his experience in college activism. We owe much of this attention to individual needs to the historical development of safe spaces.

A real concern for the activist left is that safe spaces might be institutionalized and used against the very people that created them. Should safe spaces be appropriated from activism into institutional policy, we risk something like the replacement of unions with a corporate conflict resolution center. This is unlikely to happen because safe spaces are a theoretical framework for political organizing, not a problem-solving policy. The few attempts to codify safe spaces have been in "diversity workshops" led at university orientations, and by the definitions created by critics themselves. But even in these examples, safe spaces have not been offered as solutions to problems so much as communities in which to discuss them and delve into the nuanced ways in which they impact individuals. They have been places of tension, joy, and discomfort, not places in which we declare institutional oppression resolved through a conversation. Emotions are fluid, evolving, intangible. They do not disappear at the end of a workshop. So if "the current movement is largely about well-being," it's because every political movement is. Jean Stead, a former news editor at The Guardian, recalls the blatant emotionality of Greenham Common, as women confronted by the police were "hugging each other, singing and crying." They may have appeared more "fearful" than their male counterparts, but they built a resistance and model for egalitarianism that survived generations, to the benefit of all genders.

Understanding Safe Spaces Means Understanding Privilege

HeJin Kim

HeJin Kim is an activist, human rights advocate and writer based in Cape Town, South Africa. Kim has worked with organizations like the AIDS and Rights Alliance for Southern Africa and Gender DynamiX, the first Africa-based group dedicated to the transgender community.

There is this quote, which I have been unable to find a source for anywhere: *when you're accustomed to privilege, equality feels like oppression.* No example is more proof of this than any discussion around the creation of safe spaces in the context of race, gender, sexuality, class, etc. Since I can remember I have gotten myself into conversations defending safe spaces that were women's only, trans only, people of colour only, etc. And in each instance reactions came of reverse racism and "exclusionary politics". The opposite also is very common, especially when it comes to TERF* spaces (i.e. trans women's exclusion in women's spaces), where then the right of a "safe space" from "men" is flaunted, ignoring the problematic and violent discourse behind trans exclusion and how it is perpetuated. Some people might argue that there is something illogical, or hypocritical in my reasoning when I defend certain spaces that are "exclusionary" while denouncing others; however, there is a clear line that defines when something is a safe space, as opposed to exclusionary.

It is really important to understand the issue of privilege in order to properly contextualise why a space would be stated to be "for _____ only"; privilege is what defines whether it is exclusionary and problematic, or whether it is about creating a safe space. To provide an anecdote to this: a few years ago, the one in nine campaign – a social justice organisation working on the sexual rights of women in South Africa – organised a training which they announced to be for "women who are assigned female at birth, socialised as women, and identify as women"; this phrasing was clear, and carefully crafted at that, to exclude all permutations of transness… transwomen, transmen, non-binary trans people. Of course this led to an outcry from trans activists and organisations, which were met with a very defensive attitude. But what I want to get to is a conversation I had with a prominent (cisgender) Black feminist who is (or was at that time) affiliated with the One in Nine Campaign**; at the Q&A at an event immediately after this controversy, I asked her why One in Nine was excluding transwomen from a women's space. Her answer was that "there should be times where we should be allowed to organise in exclusion"… And here is the thing, her response completely ignored the *cisgender* privilege that was at play here; the context should be clear, transgender people are oppressed in ways *cisgender* people cannot phantom, and thus *cisgender* women – while of course facing misogyny and sexism, like any other woman – have privilege that transgender women have not. Therefore, the position that One in Nine took was trans-antagonistic, it was TERF to its fullest extend, and it was violent and problematic… as was the defense of that position.

The opposite of this, trans people organising themselves in a safe space that does not allow cisgender people to enter, is thus also different; such a space is for *those who do not have*cisgender privilege to be safe, to perhaps share, heal, or organise. Such safe spaces are necessary, yet they often elicit very problematic responses from those who posses the privilege that those safe spaces are meant to protect people from. An event organised by a Black queer woman in Cape Town called *For Black Girls Only*, drew criticism of "reverse racism" almost immediately. In fact, I recall a conversation with a white man, where he could not understand why such a racist event would be organised; what he, or any of those in the "reverse racism brigade", didn't seem to understand was the *white* privilege that this space was seeking to create a refuge from. Rhodes Must Fall, a radical Black student movement at UCT that aims to decolonise higher education, organises itself around Black Consciousness and does not allow white people to take up leadership in their spaces; their approach has been called exclusionary and racist, but it is not. In fact, in many social movements, when white people are allowed to come to meetings, one white person can drown out a hundred people of colour with their voice; white privilege emboldens white people to take up space, even if the space is clearly stated to be Black led. In such a context, it is sometimes (or, actually, *often*) simply *necessary* to create a space that is specific and safe for people of colour, for Black people***. This is not racist, it is subversion and disruption of white privilege at its very core… by denying them the power to either control the narrative in a space, or to derail it.

Such Black only, people of colour only spaces are not the same as "white only spaces"; again we need to contextualise *why* such a space was constituted. White people *have* privilege, *white* privilege, and there is no valid reason for them to create an exclusionary space. White people – when it comes to race – do not *need* a safe space, because their whiteness gives them safety. The incredulous responses from white people are in many ways an expression of white fragility; their reactions stem from an irrational fear that they, as white people, face "reverse racism". But even further than that, it often simply is a way to perpetuate white racism, and their defense of "white only spaces" are in ignorance of the fact that on any level, white people – even in South Africa – have plenty of spaces where they dominate as white people, where any person of colour who enters the space will be profiles, scrutinised, and need to justify why they entering "their" space. And there it is, the white privilege, the perpetuation of white supremacy, through white fragility and fears…

[…]

When white people equate the creation of safe space by people of colour to the racism inherent in any "whites only space" – whether through underlying attitudes in white dominated spaces, or through explicitly organising them – it shows how they experience the creation of safe spaces by people of colour as oppression. That is where the arguments of "reverse racism" stem from why people of colour create safe spaces. *To the privileged, equality feels like oppression…* and it is very much the ignorance of that privilege that leads them to feel "oppressed" while being in exactly the opposite position.

Notes

* *TERF stands for "Trans Exclusionary Radical Feminism"; it is the radical feminism that has promoted "womyn born womyn" frameworks that are inherently violent to transwomen.*

** *I would like to state that since then I have not had an in-depth discussion about this with her, and I would not preclude that her views might have changed on this.*

*** *I am using the terms* people of colour *and* Black *both, as both* For Black Girls Only *and* Rhodes Must Fall *base their definition of Black in an understanding of Black Consciousness; this understanding of – as the organiser of* For Black Girls Only *put it – "Biko Black" encompasses "people of colour". I am not implying that these terms are the same in any way, or that they should be used interchangeably, or that it is this simple. Rather, for the sake of the argument I positioned them next to each other in reference to the context of the paragraph.*

Efforts to Protect People May in Fact Weaken Them

George Lakey

George Lakey is a Quaker activist, sociologist, and writer who specializes in nonviolent revolution. A co-founder of Earth Quaker Action group, he has led 1,500 workshops on five continents.

First, let's agree that safety is a human need. Studies find that children who grow up amidst threats, violence and insecurity are less likely to thrive as grown-ups. The defensiveness induced by trauma gets in the way of creativity and the learning curve needed for achievement.

The anti-oppression movement long ago began to create safe spaces. As a gay man, I remember the first time I saw on the door of a campus office a triangle, signifying that this would be a safe place for me. Surrounded by rampant homophobia, I relaxed as I turned the doorknob.

I also took the sign on the door to be a sign of sensitivity; here might be a heterosexual ally who has empathy for my frequent encounters with prejudice, even the mild expressions that could remind me of scary or hurtful incidents. That sequence – mild expression jumping to vividly remembered hurtful incidents – later became the basis for some teachers offering to give "trigger warnings" before wading into sensitive information.

Safety is a human need, like eating. Our need to eat, however, doesn't mean we need to eat all the time. Any human need exists in balance with other needs, one of which is a sense of agency. By agency I mean knowing our power, our ability to operate in a variety of circumstances, our acceptance of the responsibility to determine the course of our own lives.

"Do 'safe spaces' and 'trigger warnings' weaken us?", by George Lakey, Waging Nonviolence, January 6, 2016. https://wagingnonviolence.org/feature/do-safe-spaces-and-trigger-warnings-weaken-us/. License Under CC BY 4.0 International.

"Don't help me," my six-year-old granddaughter sometimes says, as she wrestles with a challenging task and sees me preparing to intervene. Ella knows the delicious satisfaction of her own agency and is impatient with the well-meaning, but clumsy "helping" some grown-ups are prone to. She is on her way to being a high-achieving powerhouse, like Wonder Woman, her favorite character. I've learned in the swimming pool that the scariness of water generates fears Ella wants to handle; it would be no favor to protect her. I stay nearby while she takes the risks that support her power and growing self-confidence.

For this reason, I want to raise the question of whether the current preoccupation with safety and protection has gone too far.

Acknowledging the middle-class cultural theme of protection

In the early days of gay and women's liberation and the black freedom movement, we were highly critical of mainstream culture. We knew that mainstream culture was dead wrong in enforcing white supremacy, say, or misogyny, so why should we assume it was right about anything else? We gave ourselves permission to question everything.

As liberation movements grow they come under enormous pressure to accept middle-class mainstream assumptions. Their cultural critique weakens and dubious assumptions creep in unnoticed. For the anti-oppression movement, I believe that one of those assumptions is the middle-class value of over-protection. "Really good parents" in the mainstream don't allow their children to go outside unsupervised because parents show how good they are by how much they protect children from something that might happen. "Really good homemakers" use germ-killers at every opportunity because parents show how good they are by how much they protect children from something that might sicken them.

Fortunately, push-back is happening on both those fronts — first from parents who remember happy hours of childhood freedom, and second from medical people who wonder if the growth of allergies is related to the weakened immune systems of children who don't have enough germs in their lives. On both fronts, the result is over-protection that weakens children and reduces their agency. Note the subtle dynamic of class here. Protection as obligation is especially strong in the middle class, and is generalized therefore into a hierarchy: higher-status people (who of course know better) expect themselves to ensure the safety of lower-status people.

What is now called the anti-oppression movement began with a liberatory critique but now seems to have absorbed the mainstream narrative that protection is what makes higher status people "good allies." One way this plays out in workshops is that the facilitator is expected to use ground rules, their own authority, and other methods to protect and keep "safe" everyone in the group who might otherwise experience offensive behavior.

As I watch this long-term trend I wonder what's happening to the agency of oppressed people subjected to this mainstream assumption. Are marginalized individuals in a group excused from standing up for themselves and fighting out differences with other group members that might arise? Are higher-status people coming to believe that oppressed people are by definition weak or even fragile? It wouldn't be the first time that the attitudes of do-gooders diminished others, participating in the disempowerment of those they intended to help.

Many of us have lived the pro-liberation version of movements, as we came to terms with an oppressed identity or in our role as allies or both. In the 1970s, I — an "out" gay white man — taught in an Ivy League university. In my course I found more African American students showing up each semester, seeking refuge from their wider experience of dominant white norms. In the course's three-hour experiential classes and weekend retreat, minority students renewed their determination to maintain their integrity.

We had no ground rules because I had no interest in creating a germ-free environment. Oppressive behaviors including racism showed up and useful conflicts erupted; students' power — their immune systems — grew. The course became popular because I supported black students to tackle for themselves the white-dominated world, maintaining their critical stance. They, and other marginalized students, empowered themselves. One result was a degree of community that was unheard of in a course in a huge university.

The trigger warning — a second look

Liberation/empowerment trainer Daniel Hunter pointed out to me that the demand for "safe space" easily loses track of real life. Individuals seeking safety in a classroom may imagine that a racist statement or behavior is the same as actual harm or danger. They confuse subjective feeling and objective reality. The confusion is compounded when others buy in, believing that strong feelings should rule. In the name of sensitivity, a group culture can join the historical narrative that turns oppressed people into poor victims.

The group's (or teacher's) confusion here assumes that upset feelings overrule a person's innate ability to think and act well under stress. We can test this belief. If subjective feelings control us, then surely the objective experience of harm and danger prevents us from thinking and acting smartly, right?

If we believed that, we would have to re-write history. Black Lives Matters in Minneapolis would not have come back to the police precinct house in November after the white supremacists attacked them because — since they'd been shot at — it wasn't safe. The entire civil rights movement would never have happened, nor the workers movement, nor the women's or LGBT or disability rights movement. None of these waited for safety to strategize smartly and act effectively.

People can of course be brilliant while scared or hurt — unless they believe otherwise. The quickest scan of successful social movement history shows not only what a lie the belief is, but also how delighted the 1 percent must be to watch anti-oppression extremists undermine every movement within reach.

Doesn't the trigger warning expectation invite lower

expectations of ourselves and others? When the technique is institutionalized, it suggests that oppressed people are too fragile to handle symbolic representations of oppression, much less able to handle oppression in real life. In my experience, the truth is otherwise: It is usually people with privilege who are fragile and can't deal with what oppressed people often handle well. (I'm talking about class again. Sorry about that, but we do pay a price for letting the anti-oppression forces avoid interrogating their class.)

The dearth of vision in demands for 'safe space' and 'trigger warnings'

I admit I'm an elder with high expectations. I expect movements that make many demands to have a vision of what it is they seek. If the goal is to produce hot-house plants that cannot survive without the protection of others (higher-status others, of course), admit it.

My vision is of humans working to realize their full potential, supported by their cultures to act powerfully in the world to transform institutions. Folk wisdom offers a motto to guide us as we work: "Smooth seas train poor sailors." I hope for comments from readers about how we can support everyone's power to act for liberation.

Student Demands for Safe Spaces Can Be Taken Too Far

Alexander Tsesis

Alexander Tsesis is the Raymond & Mary Simon Chair in Constitutional Law and Professor of Law at the Loyola University Chicago School of Law. His books include For Liberty and Equality: The Life and Times of the Declaration of Independence and We Shall Overcome: A History of Civil Rights and The Law.

"Safe Spaces" and "Trigger Warnings"

Some student groups have advocated for the creation of designated buffer zones against hostile environments on college campuses; others argue to the contrary that safe spaces are segregated environments that do not belong on campuses.[1] The terms "safe spaces" and "trigger warnings" sometimes include a variety of common sense rules about communications in classrooms, such as having students think before speaking, being empathic when speaking about sensitive topics, and discussing students' sense of harm in response to various complex social issues.[2] "Trigger warnings" are explicit statements that certain material discussed in an academic environment might upset sensitive students, especially those who have been traumatized by such harms as rape or discrimination.[3] The administration of trigger warnings includes allowing students uncomfortable with classroom materials to leave and not participate.[4] "Safe spaces" refers to a range of environments where students join likeminded companions at particular locations on campus.

It makes sense for faculty and students to avoid misethnic or chauvinistic phrasing to better establish and maintain a vibrant, interactive environment, one that respects other members of the student body.[5] But such warnings should be voluntary and based on professors' sensibilities about the delivery of materials

"Campus Speech and Harassment," 101 Minnesota Law Review 1863(20A). Reprinted by permission.

to diverse audiences. Moreover, students' personal spaces—be it dormitory rooms, lockers, or mailboxes—are meant to provide privacy without being subject to mean-spirited verbal attacks. So too specialized student organizations—such as black student societies or women's organizations—help participants congregate for specific purposes. But these should remain open to all and not be segregated.

At university campuses around the country, certain student organizations vociferously and sometimes violently have demanded that administrators silence speakers whom they perceive to be making unwelcome and emotionally disturbing statements.[6] There is no basis in the Constitution nor statutory authorities to require universities to cater to the demands of student or faculty groups, seeking to censure speakers who are offensive, bombastic, or inappropriate, but pose no physical or educative threat. A Northwestern University professor was recently investigated and charged for sexual harassment after she published an article mocking the university's sexual harassment policy.[7] At Amherst College, some students demanded the promulgation of a campus speech code that would punish other students who had put up an "All Lives Matter" poster.[8]

Uses of "safe spaces" and "trigger warnings" to silence and censor opponents are both exclusionary and harmful to open discourse. Confusing their personal sensibilities with hate speech, some students have demanded that schools maintain safe spaces, reminiscent of hermetically sealed echo chambers of like-minded individuals.[9] These safe spaces are by design exclusive. At Scripps College in California, administrators set aside an official time and location "for people of color" and their invited allies to "decompress, discuss, grieve, plan, support each other, etc. in solidarity."[10] In places like Pomona College, which like Scripps is part of the Claremont Colleges consortium, these spaces operate on segregated bases, for the exclusive congregation of "students of color," an ambiguous term referring to historically marginalized groups, to commiserate alone.[11] The University of Connecticut has taken matters a step further, planning to offer students segregated campus housing dorms, exclusively for black students.[12] The UCLA Afrikan Student Union made the demand for a segregated safe space, on a separate dormitory floor where only black students would be permitted to live.[13] At the University of California, Berkeley, a large group of students demanded that safe spaces be set aside for students of color and other minorities. They blocked campus sidewalks, requiring pedestrians to make their way through campus along an unpaved path and menacing those who tried to break their human chain. The protestors then boycotted a store in a prominent entrance of campus, demanding it close down and vacate space for the alliance of students of color and LGBTQIIA.[14] Student leaders next moved their boisterous protest into the Associated Students of University of California Student Union, where they disrupted students who were studying.[15] Students have also made demands for racially, sexually, and ethnically segregated spaces at Amherst College; California State University, East Bay; California State University, Los Angeles; Clemson University; New York University; and at several other universities in the United States.[16] These are not simply requests for safe dormitories, where one can feel comfortable without being harassed by racist or sexist roommates,[17] but something exclusionary and detrimental to student integration. They are efforts to use university facilities without allowing disfavored persons to join. Universities would be amiss to buckle to these demands.

To the contrary, the Supreme Court has found that universities can prohibit organizations from using funds, facilities, and official channels of communication if membership is predicated on discriminatory criteria.[18] Moreover, any public university that agrees to separate persons on the basis of racial characteristics would need to explain the policy to be compelling and narrowly tailed to the evil. It is highly unlikely that any state entity could prove any such compelling reason since classroom, dorm room, or university activity segregation would perpetuate one of the greatest evils in our national history.[19]

The "trigger warnings" movement is also part of an empathic strategy to create an ostensibly more inclusive environment, but in its extreme form it also demands the repression of disfavored speech. There are no current empirical studies demonstrating the educative value of trigger warnings; indeed, they do not get at the underlying problems—such as sexism and racism—its advocates seek to alleviate.[20] While issuing trigger warnings might protect select groups from emotional distresses, they are also likely to stilt literary discussions. Furthermore, students who would upon their own demand leave class to avoid offense would likely miss valuable lecture and discussion times, which are critical to learning. The study of human character in much literature is violent and purposefully disturbing. Fyodor Dostoyefsky's *Crime and Punishment*, Homer's *Iliad*, Richard Wright's *Native Son*, Ken Kesey's *One Flew over the Cuckoo's Nest*, and Pearl Buck's *The Good Earth* come immediately to mind: all these books contain disturbing narratives. Signaling each shocking passage in them would impose the teacher's opinion and would likely increase a professor's ideological control rather than creating an environment open to discourse and student involvement. The pain depicted in these great novels is well known to promote character and cultural development; in other words, the trauma they invoke is intrinsic to the experience of reading deeply.[21] That is not to say that trigger warnings never have a place. Indeed, a professor who finds an appropriate spot, whether on a syllabus or at some point in her course, might well help facilitate learning by using them. But enforced trigger warnings are academically and, at public universities, constitutionally suspect. They raise the worrisome specter of universities imposing government viewpoints on scholars and requiring them to transmit the accepted line to students.

At some campuses—most prominently Columbia University, Oberlin College, Rutgers University, and the University of

California—students have demanded that instructors and professors issue prior warnings before embarking on materials that might set off negative associations of sexism, racism, or similar discriminations. Enterprising students attending Columbia University, one of the powerhouses of world's classical literature,[22] decided that standard texts—such as Ovid's Metamorphoses—should be taught with supplementary alerts pointing to what some may consider disturbing depictions of rape.[23] Four student members of Columbia's Multicultural Affairs Advisory Board believed Metamorphoses to be part of a body of Western canon that "contains triggering and offensive material that marginalizes student identities in the classroom," advancing "histories and narratives of exclusion and oppression."[24] The Oberlin College administration warned that even great works of literature, such as Chinua Achebe's *Things Fall Apart*, could trigger harsh feelings from "experienced racism, colonialism, religious persecution, violence, suicide, and more." These proposals have raised some effective opposition. In the wake of an Oberlin faculty protest, the administration retracted those guidelines.[25]

Other universities have also grappled with students who sought faculty warnings about content that some might find disturbing in light of historical prejudices and discriminations. For instance, at Rutgers University a group of students demanded faculty to issue trigger warnings about Virginia Woolf's *Mrs. Dalloway*, because it deals with "suicidal inclinations," and F. Scott Fitzgerald's *The Great Gatsby*, because it had "a variety of scenes that reference gory, abusive and misogynistic violence."[26] The student senate of the University of California at Santa-Barbara issued "A Resolution to Mandate Warnings for Triggering Content in Academic Settings," which sought to require pedagogues to indicate on syllabi any assignments that might cause students emotional trauma.[27] The pedagogical inopportuneness of trigger warnings delimited by special interest student groups is evident from the type of curricular changes students have promoted around the country. These demands show little understanding that literature is meant to jar and make people uncomfortable. Triggers of strong emotions, including love, happiness, and sometimes revulsion, are part of the purpose of good literature. Authors explore diverse characters, enabling the audience to better comprehend human interactions, foibles, flaws, conditions, and idiosyncrasies.

In addition, demands for exclusionary public safe spaces and encompassing trigger warnings threatens to drive wedges between students, to stifle open discussions, and to separate groups rather than drawing them together for deliberation. These modern-day censorial approaches pose a particular threat to untenured and non-tenure-track faculty members.[28] Their reluctance to broach controversial subjects will be costly to intellectual pursuits and students' abilities to engage in open classroom discussions. A less obvious harm resulting from these complaints against ordinary abrasions of human communications is the distraction from much more serious incidents of hostile discourse on university campuses.[29]

The expression of ideas, even obnoxious ones that make certain people feel uncomfortable, are not actionable; they are protected by the First Amendment.[30] A requirement that all professors include trigger warnings for emotionally charged content would no doubt chill education. Professors would be unlikely to include controversial materials in their syllabi. In the words of the American Association of University Professors:

> Some discomfort is inevitable in classrooms if the goal is to expose students to new ideas, have them question beliefs they have taken for granted, grapple with ethical problems they have never considered, and, more generally, expand their horizons so as to become informed and responsible democratic citizens. Trigger warnings suggest that classrooms should offer protection and comfort rather than an intellectually challenging education.[31]

Even classic novels, which are invaluable for pedagogy and learning, sometimes do not fare well under the subjective scrutiny of administrators and students. There is a distinction between the study of disturbing materials and repeated harassment, with only the latter being an unprotected type of discourse.[32]

Trigger warnings can no doubt be instructive when pedagogues believe they will enrich the classroom with sensitive perspectives, but where they are administrative mandates on university faculty to present specific viewpoints in classrooms or at university events, then they constitute unconstitutional censorship. It is one thing to require faculty to teach the subjects they have been assigned, and quite another to demand that they mimic the administration's favored perspectives. In ordinary government employee settings, such as those involving postal workers or government attorneys, "when public employees make statements pursuant to their official duties, the employees are not speaking as citizens for First Amendment purposes, and the Constitution does not insulate their communications from employer discipline."[33] However, the Court has also recognized in dictum that "[t]here is some argument that expression related to academic scholarship or classroom instruction implicates additional constitutional interests that are not fully accounted for by this Court's customary employee speech jurisprudence."[34] Robert Post has elaborated on this thought, writing that university faculty's role is not to simply transmit the views of university administrators but to "expand knowledge" and apply "independent professional, disciplinary standards" in order to advance students' democratic competence.[35]

[...]

Notes

1. Meera E. Deo, *Two Sides of a Coin: Safe Space & Segregation in Race/Ethnic-Specific Law Student Organizations*, 42 WASH. U. J.L. & POL'Y 83, 123 (2013).

2. Sean Darling-Hammond & Kristen Holmquist, *Creating Wise Classrooms To Empower Diverse Law Students: Lessons in Pedagogy from Transformative Law Professors*, 17 BERKELEY J. AFR.-AM. L. & POL'Y 47, 74–75 (2016).

3. *See* Jennifer Medina, Warning: *The Literary Canon Could Make Students Squirm*, N.Y. TIMES (May 17, 2014), https://www.nytimes.com/2014/05/ 18/us/warning-the-literary-canon-could-make-students-squirm.html.

4. *See id.*

5. See Mae Kuykendall & Charles Adside, III, *Unmuting the Volume: Fisher, Affirmative Action Jurisprudence, and the Legacy of Racial Silence*, 22 WM. & MARY BILL RTS. J. 1011, 1023 (2014). For a proposal to codify a broad-based statute prohibiting expressions such as unwanted catcalls, sexual commentary, and solicitation of sex that are made in public places, see Cynthia Grant Bowman, *Street Harassment and the Informal Ghettoization of Women*, 106 HARV. L. REV. 517, 575–76 (1993).

6. See Wendy Kaminer, *The Progressive Ideas Behind the Lack of Free Speech on Campus*, WASH. POST (Feb. 20, 2015), http://www.washingtonpost.com/opinions/the-progressive-ideas-behind-the-lack-of-free-speech-on-campus/2015/02/20/93086efe-b0e7-11e4-886b-c22184f27c35_story.html.

7. *Professors Cannot Fully Participate in Student Activism*, WELLESLEY NEWS (Mar. 16, 2016), https://thewellesleynews.com/2016/03/16/professors-cannot-fully-participate-in-student-activism.

8. Nina Burleigh, Fightin' Words, NEWSWEEK, June 3, 2016, at 24, 30; Matt Johnson, *The Rapid Decline of Free Expression on Campus*, TOPEKA CAPITAL-J. (June 11, 2016), http://cjonline.com/opinion/2016-06-11/matt-johnson-rapid-decline-free-expression-campus.

9. *See, e.g.*, Scott Jaschik, *Oberlin President Says No to Students' Demands*, PBS NEWSHOUR: THE RUNDOWN (Jan. 22, 2016), http://www.pbs.org/ newshour/rundown/oberlin-president-says-no-to-black-students-demands. A curious point about the Oberlin demands was that they were not only filled with hubris about the rightness of the students' position, about such matters as whom the university should fire and whom they should promote, but also contained an element of bias. The only country the Oberlin student activists targeted was a democracy, demanding the boycott of Israel, while making no similar demand for any gross human rights abusers, such as Iran, Afghanistan, or Syria. *See* Memorandum to Bd. of Tr., President, Vice President, Oberlin College (Jan. 2016), https://new.oberlin.edu/petition-jan2016.pdf. To my mind, the only reason for such an irrational focus on Israel stems from its Jewish character and the historical stereotype of Jews being the predominant source of evil in the world. *See* KENNETH L. MARCUS, JEWISH IDENTITY AND CIVIL RIGHTS IN AMERICA 180 (2010). On the assertions of blatantly antisemitic sentiments at Oberlin, see Jeffrey Salkin, *No 'Safe Space' at Oberlin for Jewish Students Who Back Israel*, RELIGION NEWS SERV. (Mar. 8, 2016), http://religionnews.com/2016/03/08/178630.

10. Steven Glick, *Safe Spaces Segregate the Claremont Colleges*, CLAREMONT INDEP. (Nov. 17, 2015), http://claremontindependent.com/safe-spaces-segregate-the-claremont-colleges.

11. *Id.*

12. Cody Derespina, *University Living Space Gives Priority to Black Male Students, Sparking Controversy*, FOX NEWS (Feb. 2, 2016), http://www.foxnews.com/us/2016/02/02/uconn-building-black-only-living-space-to-promote-scholarship.html.

13. *Afrikan Student Union at UCLA Releases Demands,* NOMMO (Oct. 23, 2015), http://nommomagazine.com/?p=2580.

14. LGBTQIIA is an acronym that stands for: Lesbian, Gay, Bisexual, Transgender/ Transsexual, Queer/Questioning, Intersex, Intergender, Asexual.

15. Lukas Mikelionis, *Berkeley Protesters Demand 'Spaces of Color,' Harass White Students Trying To Pass,* FOX NEWS U.S. (Oct. 24, 2016), http://www.foxnews.com/us/2016/10/24/berkeley-protesters-demand-spaces-color-harass-white-students-trying-to-pass.html.

16. *Our Demands,* BLACK LIBERATION COLLECTIVE, http://www.blackliberationcollective.org/our-demands (last visited Apr. 4, 2017).

17. In a recent Internet post, Mark Tushnet suggested it is "basically quite stupid" for a university to deny students safe spaces. Mark Tushnet, *More on the University of Chicago Letter on "Safe Spaces"* [I], BALKINIZATION (Aug. 27, 2016), http://balkin.blogspot.com/2016/08/more-on-university-of-chicago-letter-on.html. As a *reductio ad absurdum*, he asserts that if such a policy were in place, university housing administrators would be prohibited or simply unwilling to respond to the complaint of a person with an offensive roommate who requested to move to different, less acrimonious accommodations. *Id.* But Tushnet's post does not provide any examples of actual student requests for safe spaces, and therefore misses the racially exclusionary nature of actual student requests for safe spaces.

18. See Christian Legal Soc'y Chapter of Univ. of Cal., Hastings Coll. of Law v. Martinez, 561 U.S. 661, 662, 697 (2010) (finding a university could reasonably require a religious student organization to comply with its nondiscrimination policy imposed on officially recognized student organizations).

19. Looking to precedents for guidance, it is unlikely such university segregation would be upheld given that even a state's attempt to segregate persons to diminish the risk of gang violence in jails was deemed to be insufficiently compelling to overcome the strict scrutiny standard. Cf. Johnson v. California, 543 U.S. 499, 504–05, 509 (2005) (overruling the court of appeals for not applying strict scrutiny, where the court of appeals applied a more deferential standard and discussed the issue being a "close case" even under that deferential standard). State-created spaces for campus segregation is less compelling because it does not involve any possibility of physical violence.

20. LORNA VERALDI & DONNA M. VERALDI, IS THERE A RESEARCH BASIS FOR REQUIRING TRIGGER WARNINGS? 1, 6–7 (2015), http://www.forensicpsychology.org/VeraldiVeraldiTriggerWarningsHandout.pdf ("Instead of a futile and chilling crusade to rid the curriculum of potential trauma triggers, American colleges and universities seeking to help traumatized students find treatment for PTSD would do well to focus on insuring that they do not face such obstacles in getting the assistance they need to begin to heal their wounds.").

21. See Laurie Essig, *Trigger Warnings Trigger Me,* CHRON. HIGHER EDUC. (Mar. 10, 2014), http://chronicle.com/blogs/conversation/2014/03/10/ trigger-warnings-trigger-me ("Trigger warnings are a very dangerous form of censorship because they're done in the name of civility. Learning is painful. It's often ugly and traumatic. How different my life would be if I hadn't read *Crime and Punishment*

because it's misogynist and violent. How terrible my teaching would be if I hadn't spent years researching spectacle lynchings and eugenics and freak shows in order to teach courses on race and American culture.").

22. *Ranking of Best Graduate English Programs*, U.S. NEWS & WORLD REP., http://grad-schools.usnews.rankingsandreviews.com/best-graduate-schools/top-humanities-schools/english-rankings (last visited Apr. 4, 2017).

23. Michael E. Miller, *Columbia Students Claim Greek Mythology Needs a Trigger Warning*, WASH. POST. (May 14, 2015), https://www.washingtonpost.com/news/morning-mix/wp/2015/05/14/columbia-students-claim-greek-mythology-needs-a-trigger-warning.

24. *Id.*

25. Colleen Flaherty, *Trigger Unhappy*, INSIDE HIGHER ED (Apr. 14, 2014), https://www.insidehighered.com/news/2014/04/14/oberlin-backs-down-trigger-warnings-professors-who-teach-sensitive-material.

26. Tony Allen-Mills, *'Gory' Gatsby Is Too Violent for US Students*, SUNDAY TIMES (Apr. 27, 2014), http://www.thesundaytimes.co.uk/sto/news/world_news/Americas/article1404301.ece; Valerie Strauss, *What 'Trigger Warning' Would the Bible Get?*, WASH. POST (May 23, 2014), https://www.washingtonpost.com/news/answer-sheet/wp/2014/05/23/what-trigger-warning-would-the-bible-get.

27. For a statement of the UC-Santa Barbara student who initiated thestudent resolution, see Bailey Loverin, *Trigger Warnings at UCSB*, DAILY NEXUS (Mar. 11, 2014), http://dailynexus.com/2014-03-11/trigger-warnings-at-ucsb.

28. Elizabeth Freeman et al., Trigger Warnings Are Flawed, INSIDE HIGHER ED (May 29, 2014), https://www.insidehighered.com/views/2014/05/29/essay-faculty-members-about-why-they-will-not-use-trigger-warnings.

29. *See* Erica Goldberg, *Free Speech Consequentialism*, 116 COLUM. L. REV. 687, 753 (2016) ("Suppressing or chilling speech with trigger warnings because of its communicative, nonconduct harms [to emotions] necessarily prioritizes the emotions of some over others in an unavoidably subjective way that may serve as a pretext for viewpoint discrimination instead of alleviating tangible harm.").

30. Keyishian v. Bd. of Regents, 385 U.S. 589, 603 (1967) ("Our Nation is deeply committed to safeguarding academic freedom, which is of transcendent value to all of us and not merely to the teachers concerned. That freedom is therefore a special concern of the First Amendment, which does not tolerate laws that cast a pall of orthodoxy over the classroom."); *cf.* City of Houston v. Hill, 482 U.S. 451, 472 (1987) ("[T]he First Amendment recognizes, wisely we think, that a certain amount of expressive disorder not only is inevitable in a society committed to individual freedom, but must itself be protected if that freedom would survive.").

31. On Trigger Warnings, AM. ASS'N U. PROFESSORS (Aug. 2014), https://www.aaup.org/report/trigger-warnings.

32. *See infra* Part II.A.4.

33. Garcetti v. Ceballos, 547 U.S. 410, 421 (2006).

34. *Id.* at 425.

35. ROBERT C. POST, DEMOCRACY, EXPERTISE, AND ACADEMIC FREEDOM: A FIRST AMENDMENT JURISPRUDENCE FOR THE MODERN STATE 92 (2012).

Safe Spaces Must Evolve to Allow for Reasoned Discourse

Sabin Densmore

Writer, designer and researcher Sabin Densmore has a Master's degree in education and often guest lectures on design theory and philosophy for educators in graduate classes. He blogs at OneGecko.com.

The concept of "Safe Space" needs to be evolved to ensure that ideas are heard in full, to ensure that people are protected from attacks because of their ideas, and to make it clear that ideas are not protected from counter arguments free from ad hominem attacks.

Before I get too far into this, I want to make note of the fact that I'm aware that my thoughts on this topic are likely to upset somebody. I'm okay with that. It's part of the process of discussion. Without negative reaction to opinions, we exist in an echo chamber. One of the problems with discourse in this country is the existence of and heavy reliance on echo chambers to enhance ideas without actually subjecting them to rational discourse. So. All of that being said, I think that the meaning and implementation of "Safe Space" needs to be adjusted so that meaningful discourse can be had about issues that affect us.

What we have ended up accomplishing as a nation is — for each faction — interpreted the First Amendment to protect the speech we agree with, but not the speech of dissent. Conservatives look to drown out Liberal ideas, and Liberals do the same to Conservatives. Economic issues are pitted against racial injustice, and men's issues become the polar opposite to feminism (they're not). Rather than be willing to recognize everyone's speech as protected, we seek to diminish the speech of others without actually *listening* to what they have to say. Consequently, the arguments lose the plot and become focused on the semantics of arguing rather than the topic of discussion. Additionally, the unwillingness to listen to others and the resulting feeling of not being heard contribute to deeper divisions between what, in many cases, are not polar opposite viewpoints, but nuanced facets of shared problems.

The First Amendment of the United States Constitution guarantees protection of speech and religion, so this argumentative discourse and shouting match is both constitutionally and legally protected. What the First Amendment doesn't guarantee is the right to be heard. This is interesting because the act of speaking implies that there is a resultant act of listening. That's what speaking is, what language is. It is a communicative act that transmits ideas through common symbols or sounds to a receiver. But what if nobody is receiving? One of the most effective ways of overcoming speech is to not listen to it, and this has become a common refrain: "If you don't like it, don't listen." But if nobody is listening, then nobody is speaking.

It was understood by implication that free speech in a democratic society is speech that is allowed as part of a public discourse, and it is in this spirit that I believe the First Amendment applies. As citizens of the United States, we are free to proclaim our opinions on any topic imaginable, and in most cases those opinions cannot be used to imprison or otherwise curtail us. There are certain precedents and nuances here, of course. If speech incite violent acts, or in cases of slander and libel someone's reputation is harmed or life is threatened, the speaker can be held liable. Those moments notwithstanding, we can pretty much say what we want. And we do.

So what does this have to do with "safe spaces"? In current practice, a safe space is a zone established where opinions are not challenged. It's usually a phrase used be Liberals or their allies, and often appears on college campuses. It's a place where a conversation can be fostered without fear of negativity, reprisals, or arguments.

It's also a place free from insults, slander, and violence. Some people see safe spaces as having great value in terms of counseling, group therapy, school assemblies, and social work: people sometimes need to be assured that what they say will not come back to harm them. Others see them as a place that can be used to foster echo chambers, to isolate opinions from counter arguments, and further entrench erroneous or naive ideas. To me, they represent both.

The kind of discourse that our nation has devolved into using is what has prompted the increase —as I see it — call for safe spaces. We have transformed the First Amendment into a protection of argumentative insults and interruptions rather than a protection of reasoned discourse where people's ideas are heard and discussed on their merits. Creating safe spaces that keep this from happening aren't doing us any favors, though. The safe space simply removes the harmful elements from the conversation but doesn't outwardly make clear that dissenting opinions are welcome. Maybe some spaces do welcome dissent, but certainly that's not the impression created with their creation.

I would like to see it established very clearly that a safe space is a place where people are safe from insulting language, personal attacks, and degradation. I would like to see it stated that a safe space is a place where people's ideas are heard on their merit, rather than shut down or shouted over. In a civil society, there should be no need for such a protection, but that's where we are right now. I do not believe a safe space should protect people from opposing viewpoints and challenges to their beliefs. People should be willing to accept that their belief systems will be questioned. They should feel safe that they will not be personally assaulted for their beliefs, but nothing should be considered sacrosanct.

This is not to say that there shouldn't be times when people of a like mind can get together and reinforce their ideas and beliefs without challenge. We need to be around people who share our opinions, and there needs to be time for those opinions to be fostered. Private meetings, faith-based meetings, rallies, and other gatherings of like-minded people should have a reasonable expectation of isolation and freedom to develop their shared ideas. Once in public, those ideas should be allowed to be expressed. And once expressed, those ideas are open to discussion, counter arguments, and debate.

In short, then, I think the idea of safe space needs to be evolved into one that provides for the safe dissemination and receipt of ideas with assurances that people are safe from insult and attempts at blocking their speech. Private meetings with like-minded people should be protected from interruption and harassment because we all need to be recharged with people who share our beliefs and ideas.

Practically speaking, an implementation of this recommendation would involve pundits on network and cable news being replaced by experts with opposing or counter viewpoints. It would involve open debates on campuses where issues are presented in a moderated format and discussion remains civil. It would involve that each community welcome all opinions about political, social, and economic ideas without ridiculing the person delivering those ideas. It would involve Facebook friends not blocking each other for opposing viewpoints. It would involve each of us examining our own opinions and beliefs in light of opposing viewpoints that we've heard. It would involve humility and destruction of ego in the face of other people's ideas. Most of all, it would require empathy: the ability to truly understand somebody else's viewpoint and how our own beliefs may be impacting that other person.

Organizations to Contact

The editors have compiled the following list of organizations concerned with the issues debated in this book. The descriptions are derived from materials provided by the organizations. All have publications or information available for interested readers. This list was compiled on the date of publication of the present volume; the information provided here may change. Be aware that many organizations take several weeks or longer to respond to inquiries, so allow as much time as possible.

American Association of University Professors (AAUP)
1133 Nineteenth St., NW, Suite 200
Washington, DC 20036
phone: (201) 737-5900
email: aaup@aaup.org
website: www.aaup.org

The AAUP is a nonprofit membership association of faculty and other academic professionals. Headquartered in Washington, DC, they have members and chapters based at colleges and universities across the country. The AAUP helps to shape American higher education by developing the standards and procedures that maintain quality in education and academic freedom in this country's colleges and universities.

American Association of University Women (AAUW)
1310 L St. NW, Suite 1000
Washington, DC 20005
phone: (800) 326-2289
email: connect@aauw.org
website: www.aauw.org

AAUW has been empowering women as individuals and as a community since 1881. They work as a national grassroots organization to improve the lives of millions of women and their families. They conduct research into gender equity issues in education and in the workplace and advocate for policies that improve the lives of girls and women. They also support challenges to discrimination of women in education and the workplace. The AAUW website includes articles on women's studies, including a number of pieces on sexist microaggressions.

American Civil Liberties Union (ACLU)

125 Broad Street,
18th Floor
New York, NY 10004
phone: (212) 549-2500
website: www.aclu.org

For nearly 100 years, the American Civil Liberties Union (ACLU) has been a guardian of liberty, working in courts, legislatures, and communities to defend and preserve the individual rights and liberties that the Constitution and the laws of the United States guarantee. Whether it's achieving full equality for LGBT people, establishing new privacy protections for our digital age of widespread government surveillance, ending mass incarceration, or preserving the right to vote or the right to have an abortion, the ACLU takes up the toughest civil liberties cases and issues to defend all people from government abuse and overreach.

American Psychological Association (APA)

750 First Street, NE
Washington, DC 20002-4242
phone: (800) 374-2721
website: www.apa.org

APA is the leading scientific and professional organization representing psychology in the United States, with more than 115,700 researchers, educators, clinicians, consultants and students as its members. Their mission is to advance the creation, communication and application of psychological knowledge to benefit society and improve people's lives.

Anti-Defamation League (ADL)
605 Third Avenue
New York, NY 10158
phone: (212) 885-7970
email: newyork@adl.com
website: www.adl.org

Founded in 1913, the Anti-Defamation League is a US civil rights/human relations organization. As a nonprofit, nonpartisan organization with supporters and partners throughout the United States and around the world, ADL speaks up for those whose voices are not always heard. Their website contains a host of materials on relevant subjects, including a high school unit on "Microaggressions in our Lives."

Gay Alliance
100 College Avenue #100
Rochester, NY 14607
email: info@gayalliance.org
website: www.gayalliance.org

The goal of the Gay Alliance is to encourage all of our social systems to become inclusive and welcoming to lesbian, gay, bisexual, transgender, queer/questioning (LGBTQ) and allied individuals. The Gay Alliance has 43 years of experience offering LGBTQ education and through their trainings they make presentations to a wide variety of clients all around the country. Their website has materials relating to LGBTQ rights, and, in particular, information about creating safe spaces.

Gay, Lesbian, and Straight Education Network
(GLSEN)
92 Broad Street
2nd Floor
New York, New York 10004
phone: (212) 727-0135
email: glsen@glsen.org
website: www.glsen.org

The Gay, Lesbian, and Straight Education Network seeks to provide a safe and healthy school environment where students of all sexual orientations are respected. GLSEN is the oversight organization for over four thousand Gay-Straight Alliance clubs in schools across the nation. They also provide Safe Space kits to schools and run a "Spot the Sticker" campaign, where rainbow–colored stickers indicate LGBTQ-friendly areas in schools.

Human Rights Watch
350 Fifth Avenue, 34th floor
New York, NY 10118-3299
phone: (212) 290-4700
email: hrwpress@hrw.org
website: www.hrw.org

Human Rights Watch is a nonprofit, nongovernmental human rights organization with offices around the world. Its staff consists of human rights professionals including country experts, lawyers, journalists, and academics of diverse backgrounds and nationalities. Established in 1978, Human Rights Watch is known for its accurate fact-finding, impartial reporting, effective use of media, and targeted advocacy, often in partnership with local human rights groups.

National Association for the Advancement of Colored
People (NAACP)
4805 Mt. Hope Drive
Baltimore, MD 21215
phone: (877) NAACP-98
email: washingtonbureau@naacpnet.org
website: www.naacp.org

The mission of the National Association for the Advancement of
Colored People is to ensure the political, educational, social, and
economic equality of rights of all persons and to eliminate race-
based discrimination. The NAACP envisions a society in which
all individuals have equal rights without discrimination based
on race. The website includes information on education, health,
and racial issues.

National Education Association (NEA)
1201 16th Street, NW
Washington, DC 20036-3290
phone: (202) 833-4000
website: www.nea.org

The National Education Society is America's largest teacher's
organization, made up of thousands of professionals from all over
the country. NEA's three million members work at every level of
education—from pre-school to university graduate programs—to
ensure that every student receives a quality education. Their website
has an extensive collection of articles about working with students
who have been subjected to trauma and creating safe spaces for
students in educational settings.

Bibliography

Books

Mahzarin R. Banaji and Anthony G. Greenwald. *Blindspot: Hidden Biases of Good People.* New York, NY: Delacorte Press, 2013.

Frank Furedi. *What's Happened to the University?: A Sociological Exploration of Its Infantilisation.* London, UK and New York, NY: Routledge, Taylor & Francis Group 2017.

Sarah Glazer. *Free Speech on Campus: Where Should Colleges Draw the Line?* Washington DC: CQ Press, 2015.

Scott Greer. *No Campus for White Men: The Transformation of Higher Education into Hateful Indoctrination.* Washington, DC: WND Books, 2017.

Mick Hume. *Trigger Warning: Is the Fear of Being Offensive Killing Free Speech?* London, UK: William Collins, 2015.

Emily J. M. Knox. *Trigger Warnings.* Lanham, MD: Rowman & Littlefield, 2017.

Greg Lukianoff. *Freedom from Speech.* New York, NY: Encounter Books, 2014.

Kevin L Nadal. *That's so Gay! Microaggressions and the Lesbian, Gay, Bisexual, and Transgender Community.* Washington, DC: American Psychological Association, 2014.

Bill O'Reilly and Bruce Feirstein. *Old School: Life in the Sane Lane.* New York, NY: Henry Holt and Company, 2017.

John G. Palfrey. *Safe Spaces, Brave Spaces: Diversity and Free Expression in Education.* Cambridge, MA, M.I.T. Press, 2017.

Mark A. Pierce. *Microaggressions Across the Great Divide: High-Stakes Written Assessments, the Threat of Stereotype and Hidden Curriculum.* Pittsburgh, PA: Rosedog Books, 2011.

Cornelia Roux. *Human Rights Education in Diverse Contexts.* Boston, MA: Sense Publishers, 2012.

Cody J. Sanders. *Microaggressions in Ministry: Confronting the Hidden Violence of Everyday Church.* Louisville, KY: Westminster John Knox Church, 2015.

Benjamin E. Sasse. *The Vanishing American Adult: Our Coming-of-*

Age-Crisis and How to Rebuilt a Culture of Self-Reliance. New York, NY: St. Martin's Press, 2017.

Tom Slater. *Unsafe Space: The Crisis of Free Speech on Campus.* London, UK: Palgrave Macmillan, 2016.

Derald Wing Sue and David Sue. *Counseling the Culturally Diverse: Theory and Practice.* Hoboken, NJ: Wiley, 2016.

Derald Wing Sue. *Microaggressions in Everyday Life: Race, Gender, and Sexual Orientation.* Hoboken, NJ: Wiley, 2013.

Annemarie Vaccaro, Gerri August and Megan S. Kennedy. *Safe Spaces: Making Schools and Communities Welcoming to LGBT Youth.* Santa Barbara, CA: Praeger, 2012.

Jonathan Zimmerman. *Campus Politics: What Everyone Needs to Know®.* New York, NY: Oxford University Press, 2016.

Periodicals and Internet Sources

Michelle Bentley, "Scenes of a Disturbing Nature: Trigger Warnings," *Critical Studies on Security*, 4 1, 2016. 114-117.

E.A. Beverly, S. Díaz, A.M. Kerr, J.T. Balbo, et al, "Students' Perceptions of Trigger Warnings in Medical Education," *Teaching and Learning in Medicine.* 2017. 1-10.

Hannah Black, Dawn L. Martin, Osita Nwanevu, et al. "Safe Spaces," *Harper's*, March 2016. 11-22.

Wendy Bostwick and Amy Hequembourg, "'Just a Little Hint': Bisexual-specific Microaggressions and Their Connection to Epistemic Injustices," *Culture, Health & Sexuality.* 16,.5. 2014. 488-503.

Guy A. Boysen, Anna M. Wells, and Kaylee J. Dawson. "Instructors' Use of Trigger Warnings and Behavior Warnings in Abnormal Psychology." *Teaching of Psychology.* 43.4. 2016. 334-339.

K. Byron. "From Infantilizing to World Making: Safe Spaces and Trigger Warnings on Campus." *Family Relations.* 66.1. 2017. 116-125.

Stephanie M. Crumpton. "Trigger Warnings, Covenants of Presence, and More: Cultivating Safe Space for Theological Discussions About Sexual Trauma." *Teaching Theology & Religion.* 20.2. 2017. 137-147.

J. Dilevko. "The Politics of Trigger Warnings." *Journal of Information*

Ethics. 24.2. 2015. 9-12. Eleanor A. Lockhart. "Why Trigger Warnings Are Beneficial, Perhaps Even Necessary." *First Amendment Studies.* 50.2. 2016. 59-69.

Tina Fetner. Athena Elafros, Sandra Bortolin, and Coralee Drechsler. "Safe Spaces: Gay-Straight Alliances in High Schools." *Canadian Review of Sociology/revue Canadienne De Sociologie.* 49.2. 2012. 188-207

Rebecca Flintoft and Christopher Bollinger. "Beyond Trigger Warnings: Preparing for Engaged Learning Within an Ethic of Care." *About Campus.* 21.3. 2016. 24-31.

Jack Halberstam. "Trigger Happy: from Content Warning to Censorship." *Signs.* 42.2. 2017. 535-542.

Virginia W. Huynh. "Ethnic Microaggressions and the Depressive and Somatic Symptoms of Latino and Asian American Adolescents." *Journal of Youth and Adolescence : a Multidisciplinary Research Publication.* 41.7. 2012. 831-846.

K.C. Kritikos. "Thoughts on Trigger Warnings: Spoiler Alerts at Best and Censorship at Worst?" *Journal of Information Ethics.* 25.2. 2016. 14-15

Roxana Llerena-Quinn. "A Safe Space to Speak Above the Silences." *Culture, Medicine and Psychiatry.* 37.2. 2013. 340-346.

Alexis Lothian. "Choose Not to Warn: Trigger Warnings and Content Notes from Fan Culture to Feminist Pedagogy." *Feminist Studies.* 42.3. 2016. 743-756.

Althea Nagai. "The Pseudo-Science of Microaggressions." *Academic Questions.* 30.1. 2017. 47-57

Sonny Nordmarken. "Microaggressions." *Transgender Studies Quarterly.* 1. 2014. 129-134.

Petro du Preez. "The "human Right" to Education, the Ethical Responsibility of Curriculum, and the Irony in "safe Spaces"." *Promoting Changes in Times of Transition and Crisis: Reflections on Human Rights Education.* 2013. 407-420.

S.P. Robbins. "From the Editor—Sticks and Stones: Trigger Warnings, Microaggressions, and Political Correctness." *Journal of Social Work Education.* 52.1. 1-5.

Elissa Sarno and A J. Wright. "Homonegative Microaggressions and Identity in Bisexual Men and Women." *Journal of Bisexuality.* 13.1. 2013. 63-81.

Edward Sellman. "Safe Spaces, Support, Social Capital: a Critical Analysis of Artists Working with Vulnerable Young People in Educational Contexts." *International Journal of Art & Design Education*. 34.1. 2015. 60-72

Derald W. Sue, Kevin L. Nadal, Christina M. Capodilupo, et al. "Racial Microaggressions against Black Americans: Implications for Counseling." *Journal of Counseling & Development*. 86.3. 2008. 330-338.

Richard E. Vatz. "The Academically Destructive Nature of Trigger Warnings." *First Amendment Studies*. 50.2. 2016. 51-58.

Wendy Wyatt. "The Ethics of Trigger Warnings." *Teaching Ethics*. 16.1. 2016. 17-35.

Index